New Immigrants, Changing Communities

New Immigrants, Changing Communities

Best Practices for a Better America

Elżbieta M. Goździak and Micah N. Bump

LEXINGTON BOOKS

A division of
ROWMAN & LITTLEFIELD PUBLISHERS, INC.
Lanham • Boulder • New York • Toronto • Plymouth, UK

LEXINGTON BOOKS

A division of Rowman & Littlefield Publishers, Inc.
A wholly owned subsidiary of The Rowman & Littlefield Publishing Group, Inc.
4501 Forbes Boulevard, Suite 200
Lanham, MD 20706

Estover Road
Plymouth PL6 7PY
United Kingdom

British Library Cataloguing in Publication Information Available

Library of Congress Cataloging-in-Publication Data
Goździak, Elżbieta M., 1954–
　New immigrants, changing communities : best practices for a better
　　　America / Goździak, Elżbieta and Micah N. Bump.
　　p. cm.
　Includes index.
　ISBN-13: 978-0-7391-0634-1 (cloth : alk. paper)
　ISBN-13: 978-0-7391- 0637-2 (pbk. : alk. paper)
　ISBN-10: 0-7391-0634-1 (cloth : alk. paper)
　ISBN-10: 0-7391-0637-6 (pbk. : alk. paper)
　1. Immigrants—United States—Social conditions. 2. United States—
　Emigration and immigration—Social aspects. 3. Assimilation (Sociology)
　4. Minorities—United States—Social conditions. 5. United States—Ethnic
　relations. I. Bump, Micah N., 1978– II. Title.
　JV6450.G68 2008
　304.8'73—dc22　　　　　　　　　　　　　　　　　　2008002217

Printed in the United States of America

♾™ The paper used in this publication meets the minimum requirements of
American National Standard for Information Sciences—Permanence of Paper
for Printed Library Materials, ANSI/NISO Z39.48-1992.

Contents

Acknowledgments

This handbook would have not been possible without the support and collaboration of a great many people. Our heartfelt appreciation goes out to a private foundation that wishes to remain anonymous for providing generous financial support to carry out the original research on immigrant integration in new settlement areas. The findings of that study were presented in a volume of case studies, *Beyond the Gateway: Immigrants in a Changing America*, edited by Elżbieta M. Goździak and Susan F. Martin and published by Lexington Books in 2005. The research enabled us to identify the promising practices presented in this volume. Many thanks to the Carnegie Corporation of New York for providing us with a grant to carry out a series of training programs based on the original research and to compile this handbook. We are particularly grateful to Geraldine P. Mannion, our project officer at the Carnegie Corporation, for her enthusiastic support as we were translating our research into action and gathering information about promising integration strategies.

At Georgetown University, Susan F. Martin, the executive director of the Institute for the Study of International Migration (ISIM), has unflaggingly provided guidance in a hundred great and small ways at every step of this project, from securing funding for the effort to providing comments on the final drafts of the handbook. Andrew Schoenholtz, ISIM's deputy director, was also invaluable. In fact, his research on immigrant homeownership and the ensuing handbook *Reaching the Immigrant Market: Creating Homeownership Opportunities for New Americans* served as inspiration for this publication. B. Lindsay Lowell, ISIM's director of policy research, also provided valuable input to both the original research project and this product. And last but not least, many thanks to ISIM's research assistants, Tabassum Siraj and Darcie Allen, for helping us with the first draft of this handbook.

The real heroes of this effort are the local community leaders and service providers who designed and implemented the promising practices and strategies described in this handbook as well as endured endless interviews and follow-up phone calls. We are thankful to each one of them. We felt particularly inspired by the leadership efforts of Katy Pitcock, the founder of Latino Connection in Winchester, Virginia. It is to Katy that we dedicate this handbook. We are sure that she will find numerous creative ways to utilize it in her work that we could not even begin to envision. Katy never ceases to amaze us.

Preface

Immigrants came to the United States in record numbers during the past 15 years. The foreign-born population grew by 16.5 million people, or 86 percent, between 1990 and 2005. According to the 2005 American Community Survey, there were approximately 36 million foreign-born residing in the U.S. in 2005, representing 12.3 percent of the total population. While the majority settled in traditional gateway communities, many moved to states that had seen few immigrants since the late 19th century. These "new settlement" areas stretch from the southeast in Georgia and North Carolina, then across the Great Plains to Nevada and Minnesota. The immigrant pioneers moving to new settlement areas tend to be Latino and to a lesser extent Asian. They are younger and have more children than natives and will remain the major force behind population growth in the United States.

The roots of the new settlement patterns are complex. In some cases, businesses actively recruited immigrants into new communities. During the 1980s, industries involved in meat processing began to relocate from north central states to south central states to recruit non-union, low-wage labor.[1] Establishing themselves in rural communities with small labor forces, processing companies have recruited immigrant workers from California and Texas as well as directly from Mexico and Central America. Such communities as Rogers, Arkansas; Georgetown, Delaware; and Faribault, Minnesota, now have sizable immigrant populations; aggressive recruitment is no longer necessary because immigrant networks attract newcomers.

Agriculture has also anchored many new settlement areas, as growers of labor-intensive crops have cast a broad net for workers. The Latinization of agriculture has characterized the apple groves of Washington State, the mushroom sheds of New England, the grape and row crops of southern

California, and the orange groves of southern Florida. The 1986 amnesty for nearly three million unauthorized workers created several settlement areas with distinct demographic and employment patterns.² Legal status created job stability if not income security, allowing families to reunite with relatives who had been living overseas and to develop stronger roots in their new communities.

In other cases, government programs have dispersed newcomers to communities with growing economies and appropriate support networks. The federal Office of Refugee Resettlement (ORR), for example, has provided grants to voluntary resettlement agencies to place newly arrived refugees in "preferred communities where there is a history of low welfare utilization and a favorable earned income potential relative to the cost of living" (ORR website). ORR has funded projects, including the relocation of unemployed Hmong refugees in the central valley of California to towns with lower unemployment rates and the resettlement of the Sudanese "Lost Boys" in areas with services for unaccompanied refugee minors. As a result of such initiatives, new immigrant communities have sprouted in places such as Fargo, North Dakota; Greensboro, North Carolina; and Lincoln, Nebraska.

Despite changes in settlement patterns, immigrants today struggle no less than their nineteenth-century predecessors with integration and the question of how to preserve their ethnic identity while fully participating in the mainstream institutions. Some scholars argue that the modern phenomena of multiculturalism and transnationalism diminish the incentives to participate in their new communities, but immigrants today still confront the tensions between defending the old and embracing the new. Particularly in new settlements with little previous exposure to immigrants, the issue also demands the attention of the host society, which must strike a balance between engaging newcomers and developing tolerance of differences.

The influx of newcomers to historically homogenous communities, unaccustomed to dealing with ethnically, linguistically, and religiously diverse minority populations, has posed significant challenges both to the immigrants and to the host communities. The newcomers have brought diverse needs, interests, and customs, and they are developing new linguistic, political, economic, and social patterns. They find themselves in strange communities where at first they might not know anyone. They may be intimidated by their new surroundings and new neighbors because of language and cultural barriers. Learning a new language is much more difficult for adults than for children. It takes time to learn English; participation in English language training must often be fit in among several part-time jobs, family duties, and childcare. Established residents too find change difficult. They are frustrated that newcomers "stick together" and do not integrate easily into the local community. Service providers—teachers, school administrators, health care providers, and law enforcement representatives—often find themselves ill-equipped to serve immigrants arriving in new settlement areas.

In 2002, the Institute for the Study of International Migration at Georgetown University embarked on a multiyear project to study immigrant integration in areas without recent experience with foreign-born newcomers. A multidisciplinary team of researchers explored opportunities, problems, and solutions to the social and economic integration of immigrants in these areas. The goal of the project was to inform policymaking and provide examples for new immigrant communities of how others have adapted to similar challenges. The core of the volume includes case studies of six new settlement areas: Rogers, Arkansas; Atlanta and Chamblee, Georgia; Greensboro, North Carolina; Twin Cities and Faribault, Minnesota; Salt Lake City and Park City, Utah; and Winchester, Virginia.

This handbook builds on the research presented in *Beyond the Gateway*. One of the objectives of the research was to identify practices facilitating or enhancing immigrant integration adopted in new settlement areas that might prove useful elsewhere, whether by easing the integration of newcomers or by mitigating the negative impacts of migration on receiving communities. The programs and strategies described in this handbook offer a glimpse into a wide array of innovative approaches developed in new settlement areas around the country. Indeed, the diversity of practices found in this localized study of six states suggests a range of approaches beyond the scope of any one handbook.

This handbook provides a review of promising practices and strategies facilitating immigrant integration identified in the course of our research. The purpose of this handbook is to foster a constructive approach to newcomers and community change. It includes descriptions of winning approaches as well as analysis of programmatic challenges. By highlighting successful initiatives in newcomer communities it seeks to assist stakeholders in their decision-making processes. However, newcomer-related issues are complex and the solutions are rarely "one size fits all." The programs described here are unique responses to particular issues in individual communities, and they may not be an exact fit in other communities. The handbook is not a cookbook or a blueprint, which can be applied anywhere and everywhere. Rather, it is meant as inspiration and motivation for trying out new strategies. Finding durable solutions to newcomer-related issues requires an ongoing effort, and we hope that this handbook will promote the exchange of ideas between communities and individuals that will facilitate newcomer integration. It is our hope that many practitioners, including service providers, community leaders, representatives of local governments, as well as funders, both public and private, will find this handbook useful.

The discussion is organized thematically around general areas in which improvements and innovations have the greatest potential to enhance integration. In the course of our fieldwork, several promising practices became apparent. These included programs facilitating English language acquisition, access to culturally sensitive and linguistically appropriate health care services, access to vocational training and higher education opportunities, community development, microenterprise, creation of homeownership opportunities for immigrants, and efforts to ensure safety of newcomers, to name a few.

NOTES

1. Michael J. Broadway and Terry Ward, "Recent Changes in the Structure and Location of the U.S. Meatpacking Industry," *Geography* 75, no. 1 (1990): 76–79.

2. B. Lindsay Lowell "Circular Mobility, Migrant Communities, and Policy Restrictions: Unauthorized Flows from Mexico," in *Migration, Population Structure, and Redistribution Policies,* ed. C. Goldheider (Boulder, Co: Westview Press, 1992), 137–58.

1

Immigrants in New Settlement Areas: A Portrait

NUMBER OF IMMIGRANTS AND ARRIVALS IN THE U.S.

There are 36 million immigrants in the United States today, with about 1 million new immigrants arriving each day. A historically high wave of immigration continues to create profound changes in the U.S. urban, suburban, and rural makeup. About 36 million foreign-born people live in the United States today, representing 12.4 percent of the total population. As Table 1.1 shows, most of the U.S. 36 million immigrants arrived after 1980. Every year, approximately 1 million new immigrants come, and there is no indication that the pace is slowing. More than 75 percent of the foreign-born population comes from Latin America or Asia. The vast majority have legal status in the United States and plan to remain permanently.

Table 1.1. Period of Arrival of the U.S. Foreign-Born Population, 2005

Period of Arrival	Percent
2000 to 2005	22
1990 to 1999	31
1985 to 1989	12
Pre-1985	35

Source: Table generated by Micah Bump of ISIM, Georgetown University. Data from the 2005 ACS IPUMS: Steven Ruggles, Matthew Sobek, Trent Alexander, Catherine A. Fitch, Ronald Goeken, Patricia Kelly Hall, Miriam King, and Chad Ronnander. Integrated Public Use Microdata Series: Version 3.0 [Machine-readable database]. Minneapolis, MN: Minnesota Population Center [producer and distributor], 2007.

1

Table 1.2. Where the Foreign Born Originate

Country	Population	Percent
1. Mexico	11,164,770	29.5
2. Philippines	1,694,586	4.5
3. India	1,425,819	3.8
4. China	1,222,513	3.2
5. Germany	1,175,274	3.1
6. Vietnam	1,091,078	2.9
7. Korea	1,039,311	2.7
8. El Salvador	994,418	2.6
9. Canada	950,021	2.5
10. Cuba	923,608	2.4
11. Dominican Republic	729,244	1.9
12. Guatemala	652,909	1.7
13. Jamaica	592,879	1.6
14. Colombia	566,394	1.5
15. Japan	517,860	1.4
16. Haiti	491,131	1.3
17. England	480,255	1.3
18. Poland	459,355	1.2
19. Italy	452,260	1.2
20. Other/USSR/Russia	395,440	1.0

Source: Same as Table 1.1.

WHERE IMMIGRANTS COME FROM

Immigrants to the United States come from every country in the world, but 20 countries currently account for more than two-thirds of the flow and five countries account for more than 40 percent. Table 1.2 indicates that many more come from Mexico than any other country. Other major countries of origin include the Philippines, the People's Republic of China, Cuba, Vietnam, Germany, India, and the Dominican Republic. In terms of source regions, Latin America accounts for more than one-half of immigrants to the United States; one-quarter come from Asia; about one-sixth come from Europe.

WHERE IMMIGRANTS SETTLE

Immigrants go where they can find jobs and live with family; they are both concentrated and dispersed. While more than 66 percent of all foreign born reside in six gateway states of California, New York, Texas, Florida, Illinois, and New Jersey, there is a growing trend toward broader dispersal across the United States. Economic conditions, such as cost of living and employment

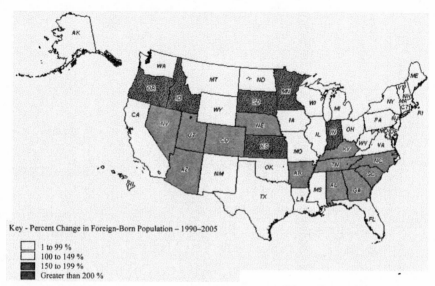

Figure 1.1. Percent Growth of Foreign-Born U.S. Population, 1990–2005
Source: U.S. Census Bureau, American Community Survey 2005.

opportunities, are increasingly motivating immigrants to move to states such as Georgia, Nevada, North Carolina, Arizona, Arkansas, and Oregon. Figure 1.1 shows that these and other non-traditional receiving states have seen significant growth in their foreign-born populations, ushering in a new era of integration challenges across the country.

DEFINING TRADITIONAL, NEW SETTLEMENT, AND MODERATE GROWTH IMMIGRANT STATES

The foreign-born population in the United States grew by 16.5 million people, or 86 percent, between 1990 and 2005. As Table 1.3 shows, all 50 states and the District of Columbia experienced an increase in their foreign-born populations during this 15-year span. This section of the handbook explores this absolute growth in terms of states, classifying them as traditional, new and moderate growth states.

TRADITIONAL STATES AVERAGED 82 PERCENT GROWTH

The largest absolute increases of the foreign-born population occurred in the traditional states of California, Florida, Illinois, New Jersey, New York,

Table 1.3.   Ranking of States: Traditional, New Settlement, and Moderate Growth States for the Foreign-Born Population—1990–2005

Traditional, New Settlement, and Moderate Growth States	1990 Population Estimate	2000 Population Estimate	2005 Population Estimate	1990 to 2000 Percent Change	2000 to 2005 Percent Change	1990 to 2005 Percent Change
Total USA	**19,192,457**	**30,760,065**	**35,689,842**	**60.3**	**16.0**	**86.0**
Traditional States						
California	6,327,076	8,809,641	9,611,356	39.2	9.1	51.9
Florida	1,487,998	2,878,503	3,542,513	93.4	23.1	97.8
Illinois	926,904	1,518,500	1,695,289	63.8	11.6	82.9
New Jersey	946,142	1,459,007	1,662,857	54.2	14.0	75.8
New York	1,624,106	2,634,349	3,212,955	62.2	22.0	44.3
Texas	2,769,166	3,819,028	3,997,268	37.9	4.7	138.1
Total	**14,081,392**	**21,119,028**	**23,722,238**	**58.5**	**14.1**	**81.8**
New Settlement States						
Alabama	39,863	86,967	120,773	118.2	38.9	203.0
Arizona	268,599	654,746	843,296	143.8	28.8	214.0
Arkansas	24,096	71,934	101,169	198.5	40.6	319.9
Colorado	137,646	367,250	460,294	166.8	25.3	234.4
Delaware	21,287	44,757	62,867	110.3	40.5	195.3
Georgia	164,953	573,161	795,419	247.5	38.8	382.2
Idaho	26,700	62,523	76,377	134.2	22.2	186.1
Indiana	91,375	186,447	242,281	104.0	29.9	165.2
Iowa	41,672	87,215	103,143	109.3	18.3	147.5
Kansas	58,964	134,470	153,535	128.1	14.2	160.4
Kentucky	29,099	74,741	98,798	156.9	32.2	239.5

Maryland	304,945	512,040	641,373	67.9	25.3	110.3
Minnesota	109,212	251,718	316,716	130.5	25.8	190.0
Mississippi	19,491	36,673	43,336	88.2	18.2	122.3
Missouri	78,532	150,003	193,735	91.0	29.2	146.7
Nebraska	25,293	71,588	96,127	183.0	34.3	280.1
Nevada	102,858	315,164	413,298	206.4	31.1	301.8
New Mexico	77,334	147,450	168,640	90.7	14.4	118.1
North Carolina	109,557	425,246	560,753	288.2	31.9	411.8
Oklahoma	61,879	126,322	155,880	104.1	23.4	151.9
Oregon	130,856	285,760	344,575	118.4	20.6	163.3
South Carolina	45,867	115,508	170,750	151.8	47.8	272.3
South Dakota	6,487	13,858	17,269	113.6	24.6	166.2
Tennessee	56,043	156,488	223,118	179.2	42.6	298.1
Utah	55,277	156,066	192,916	182.3	23.6	249.0
Virginia	300,807	561,332	723,667	86.6	28.9	140.6
Washington	309,042	608,622	750,258	96.9	23.3	142.8
Wisconsin	111,122	186,731	227,372	68.0	21.8	104.6
Total	**2,808,856**	**6,464,780**	**8,297,735**	**138.0**	**28.4**	**207.8**
Moderate Growth States						
Alaska	20,935	36,564	34,368	74.7	-6.0	64.2
Connecticut	268,726	361,122	423,254	34.4	17.2	57.5
District of Columbia	56,789	72,432	67,717	27.5	-6.5	19.2
Hawaii	160,478	209,275	212,404	30.4	1.5	32.4
Louisiana	82,704	116,364	121,590	40.7	4.5	47.0
Maine	34,884	35,524	38,727	1.8	9.0	11.0
Massachusetts	552,131	752,899	891,184	36.4	18.4	61.4
Michigan	341,550	510,966	605,656	49.6	18.5	77.3
Montana	12,224	16,087	16,734	31.6	4.0	36.9

(continues)

Table 1.3. *(continued)*

Traditional, New Settlement, and Moderate Growth States	1990 Population Estimate	2000 Population Estimate	2005 Population Estimate	1990 to 2000 Percent Change	2000 to 2005 Percent Change	1990 to 2005 Percent Change
New Hampshire	38,449	50,007	72,480	30.1	44.9	88.5
North Dakota	8,570	11,490	11,968	34.1	4.2	39.6
Ohio	246,561	338,203	387,216	37.2	14.5	57.0
Pennsylvania	347,722	495,017	603,674	42.4	22.0	73.6
Rhode Island	91,533	116,653	130,517	27.4	11.9	42.6
Vermont	15,988	21,867	21,843	36.8	-0.1	36.6
West Virginia	15,034	19,961	19,302	32.8	-3.3	28.4
Wyoming	7,931	11,826	11,235	49.1	-5.0	41.7
Total	**2,302,209**	**3,176,257**	**3,669,869**	**36.3**	**8.8**	**47.9**

Source: Table generated by Micah Bump of ISIM, Georgetown University. Estimates for 1990 and 2000 are from 5 percent IPUMS: Steven Ruggles, Matthew Sobek, Trent Alexander, Catherine A. Fitch, Ronald Goeken, Patricia Kelly Hall, Miriam King, and Chad Ronnander. Integrated Public Use Microdata Series: Version 3.0 [Machine-readable database]. Minneapolis, MN: Minnesota Population Center [producer and distributor], 2007. Data are from the IPUMS 2005 ACS.

and Texas. These traditional states recorded the highest absolute *numerical* growth in foreign-born population in the 1990s, but not the most rapid percentage growth. In fact, the growth rate of the foreign-born population in the traditional states slowed while the growth rate accelerated in the new settlement states. Although 87 percent of net foreign-born growth in the 1980s took place in the traditional states, only 60 percent of foreign-born growth occurred in those states in the 1990s.

NEW SETTLEMENT STATES SHOWED
OVER 100 PERCENT GROWTH

During the 1990s, the foreign born increasingly moved to states without a recent history of immigration. The 2005 American Community Survey data indicate that states mainly in the South and West emerged as more popular destinations than traditional states for the foreign born. Table 1.3 shows that between 1990 and 2005, 28 new settlement states experienced extremely high rates of growth, defined here as net increases in their foreign-born populations of more than 100 percent. Figure 1.1 shows that these states span a wide band in the Southeast, Midwest, and Rocky Mountain regions. The fastest growth of foreign-born population occurred in North Carolina, Georgia, and Arkansas, which experienced growth rates of 412 percent, 382 percent, and 320 percent, respectively.

MODERATE GROWTH STATES SHOWED
UNDER 100 PERCENT GROWTH

Outside of the traditional and new settlement areas, 17 states can be classified as having moderate rates of population growth. These "moderate growth" states have relatively small foreign-born populations and experienced immigrant growth rates of less than 100 percent between 1990 and 2005. Despite their lower statewide growth rates, many local communities within the moderate growth states witnessed significant increases in their foreign-born populations. They face many of the same integration challenges as the new settlement states.

SLOWER GROWTH DOES NOT MEAN SMALL NUMBERS

Although their rate of growth slowed between 1990 and 2005, traditional migration states still retain the bulk of the total foreign-born population. More than two-thirds (67 percent) of the foreign born resided in the traditional states in 2005. California alone held 27 percent of the entire foreign-born population. In contrast, new settlement states together comprised 23 percent of the national foreign-born population in 2005. The remaining 10 percent lived in the 17 moderately growing states.

SOCIOECONOMIC CHARACTERISTICS OF THE FOREIGN BORN VERSUS THE NATIVE BORN

Table 1.4 indicates that the immigrants residing in new settlement states in 2005 were more likely to be new arrivals from abroad, often in the five years leading up to the 2005 American Community Survey. Newly arrived immigrant populations often have distinctive socioeconomic characteristics that set them apart from more established immigrants. For example, they are more likely to be young males. In general, newcomer migrants in new settlement regions are more often young males, while secondary migrants who have resided in the country for longer periods of time tend to be members of family units. This casual speculation generally holds true, but there are otherwise few large socioeconomic differences between immigrants in traditional, new settlement, and moderate growth states.

IMMIGRANTS IN NEW SETTLEMENT STATES ARE YOUNG

Table 1.5 indicates that the average age of the foreign-born population varies substantially across the traditional, new settlement, and moderate growth states. The population is youngest in the new settlement states where immigrants are about six years younger than the foreign-born population in the traditional and moderate growth states. This fits with the expectation that immigrants in new settlement states are a more newly arrived and mobile population. Overall, the average age of the native-born population at mid-decade was approximately 2 years less than that of the foreign born.

Table 1.4.   Years in the U.S. of the Foreign-Born Population, 2005

Traditional, New Settlement, and Moderate Growth States	*Years in the United States*					
	0 to 5	*6 to 10*	*11 to 15*	*16 to 20*	*21+*	*Total*
Traditional States	20.1%	16.6%	14.7%	12.3%	36.3%	100.0%
New Settlement States	29.0%	19.4%	12.7%	9.5%	29.3%	100.0%
Moderate Growth States	21.6%	14.5%	10.9%	9.8%	43.2%	100.0%
Total USA	**21.8%**	**16.7%**	**14.1%**	**12.1%**	**35.2%**	**100.0%**

Source: Same as Table 1.1.

Table 1.5.   Selected Demographic and Language Characteristics by State, 2005

Traditional, New Settlement, and Moderate Growth States	Average Years of		Foreign Born		
	Foreign Born	Native Born	Male to Female Population	Speaks English Well or Better	Linguistically Isolated
Total USA	**39.3**	**37.5**	**100.3**	**0.0%**	**0.0%**
Traditional States					
California	40.0	36.6	98.6	0.7%	0.3%
Florida	43.1	35.7	94.0	0.7%	0.3%
Illinois	38.9	39.0	106.7	0.8%	0.3%
New Jersey	41.1	39.8	99.3	0.7%	0.3%
New York	42.6	42.3	93.1	0.6%	0.4%
Texas	36.7	34.6	107.7	0.8%	0.2%
Total	**40.4**	**38.0**	**99.9**	**0.0%**	**0.0%**
New Settlement States					
Alabama	34.0	37.2	106.2	0.6%	0.4%
Arizona	35.3	32.7	106.5	0.7%	0.3%
Arkansas	32.4	36.4	107.9	0.7%	0.3%
Colorado	34.5	32.8	109.7	0.7%	0.2%
Delaware	37.8	36.4	96.3	0.7%	0.3%
Georgia	34.7	33.4	118.6	0.7%	0.4%
Idaho	33.5	33.7	103.8	0.7%	0.3%
Indiana	35.0	37.8	115.3	0.7%	0.3%
Iowa	34.3	37.8	109.4	0.7%	0.3%
Kansas	34.6	35.0	115.8	0.8%	0.2%
Kentucky	37.4	35.8	113.2	0.8%	0.2%
Maryland	39.5	35.2	98.2	0.8%	0.3%
Minnesota	34.4	36.0	104.8	0.7%	0.3%
Mississippi	39.0	35.9	119.3	0.8%	0.2%
Missouri	36.3	37.6	96.7	0.7%	0.4%
Nebraska	33.3	34.2	112.5	0.7%	0.3%
Nevada	37.9	29.1	103.1	0.6%	0.4%
New Mexico	38.0	35.9	97.9	0.7%	0.4%
North Carolina	33.9	36.0	122.9	0.7%	0.3%
Oklahoma	35.0	37.6	108.3	0.7%	0.4%
Oregon	35.4	36.0	108.2	0.7%	0.3%
South Carolina	36.4	36.4	110.1	0.7%	0.4%
South Dakota	31.0	34.0	96.1	0.7%	0.3%
Tennessee	35.2	36.3	118.1	0.7%	0.3%
Utah	33.7	30.0	107.5	0.8%	0.2%
Virginia	38.4	35.7	98.4	0.8%	0.3%
Washington	37.8	35.1	94.3	0.7%	0.3%
Wisconsin	36.4	38.2	108.4	0.7%	0.3%
Total	**35.5**	**35.3**	**107.4**	**0.0%**	**0.0%**

(*continues*)

Table 1.5. *(continued)*

Traditional, New Settlement, and Moderate Growth States	Average Years of		Foreign Born		
	Foreign Born	Native Born	Male to Female Population	Speaks English Well or Better	Linguistically Isolated
Moderate Growth States					
Alaska	44.6	30.4	78.1	0.8%	0.2%
Connecticut	41.6	40.0	97.5	0.8%	0.2%
District of Columbia	37.6	34.7	94.9	0.8%	0.2%
Hawaii	45.8	35.4	71.8	0.8%	0.2%
Louisiana	41.9	37.5	99.7	0.9%	0.1%
Maine	49.2	40.5	64.9	0.8%	0.3%
Massachusetts	39.8	38.8	99.5	0.8%	0.2%
Michigan	39.1	39.0	102.3	0.9%	0.1%
Montana	47.4	38.2	60.1	0.9%	0.1%
New Hampshire	41.7	35.9	83.0	0.9%	0.2%
North Dakota	39.4	35.6	69.5	0.8%	0.2%
Ohio	40.8	39.9	96.7	0.8%	0.3%
Pennsylvania	41.0	39.8	95.8	0.7%	0.3%
Rhode Island	41.0	37.8	99.9	1.0%	0.1%
Vermont	47.0	39.0	86.0	1.0%	0.1%
West Virginia	45.9	38.1	104.3	0.8%	0.2%
Wyoming	42.9	36.1	112.5	0.8%	0.2%
Total	**42.7**	**37.4**	**89.2**	**0.0%**	**0.0%**

Source: Same as Table 1.1.

IMMIGRANT MALES OUTNUMBER FEMALES IN NEW SETTLEMENT STATES

Immigrant men slightly outnumber females, with 100.3 males for every 100 females. But Table 1.5 shows that this ratio varies across traditional, new settlement, and moderate growth states, supporting the notion that immigrants in the new settlement states are younger and more recent arrivals. Males have a greater tendency to be migratory pioneers, which is supported by the fact that in the new settlement states, where the migrants are more newly arrived, there are 107.4 males to every 100 females. In contrast, in the traditional states there are 99.9 males for every 100 females, a male deficit that is typical of settled migrant populations. The same is true in the moderate growth states, where there were 89.2 foreign-born males for every 100 foreign-born females.

ENGLISH LANGUAGE ABILITY IS LOWER IN
TRADITIONAL AND NEW SETTLEMENT STATES

Knowledge of the English language is an important indicator of integration. English language ability generally increases with the length of stay in the United States. The data in Table 1.5 show little variance in the English language ability of the foreign-born population residing in the traditional and new settlement states. In contrast, immigrants in the moderate growth states are more likely to speak English well or better than those in the traditional and new settlement states. This is explained by the fact that the foreign-born populations in the traditional and new settlement states have more recent arrivals than in the moderate growth states.

LINGUISTIC ISOLATION VARIES SOMEWHAT BETWEEN STATES

The census measure of linguistic isolation captures individuals in households where no adult speaks English at home. As with English language ability, the rate of linguistic isolation does not vary greatly among the traditional and new settlement states but is much lower in the moderate growth states. Table 1.5 shows that the new settlement states, at 30.5 percent, had the highest rate of linguistic isolation. This figure was slightly lower in traditional states, where 29.8 percent of the foreign-born population indicated that they were linguistically isolated. Only 18.2 percent of the foreign born in moderate growth states live in linguistically isolated households.

IMMIGRANTS HAVE BOTH LESS
AND MORE EDUCATION THAN NATIVES

Immigrants are most prominently represented at both ends of the educational spectrum; that is, they have either very low or very high levels of education and are less likely to have mid-level education. While this trend holds true across the three different categories of states, its extent varies depending on the type of state in question. Table 1.6 shows that overall, 31.4 percent of all immigrants above the age of 25 had less than a high school education in 2005, which is significantly higher than the 12.7 percent of natives in the same category. At 12.3 percentage points, the educational gap between the native and foreign born at the low end is smallest in the moderate growth states. This gap is 14.8 and 20.1 percentage points in the new settlement and traditional settlement states, respectively.

This gap does not exist at higher levels of education where 27 percent of both the native and the foreign-born populations have at least an under-graduate education. However, Table 1.6 shows that at the highest levels of education, a larger percentage of the foreign born have completed advanced degrees. Overall, 11.1 percent of the foreign-born population in the U.S. has an advanced degree compared to only 9.8 percent of the native population. This gap is smallest in the traditional settlement states where the two populations are separated by less than one percentage point. The difference grows to 3.7 percentage points in the new settlement states and 5.7 percentage points in the moderate growth states.

IMMIGRANTS HAVE A SLIGHTLY HIGHER LABOR FORCE PARTICIPATION RATE THAN NATIVES

The labor force participation rate measures the percentage of employed and unemployed workers in the population 16 years and older. Nationally, the foreign-born labor force participation rate is 67.1 percent, compared to 65.7 percent for the native population. As illustrated by Table 1.7, there is not much variance in labor force participation rates across the three groups of settlement states between the native and foreign-born population. The greatest difference occurs in the new settlement states, where the foreign-born labor force participation rate is 3.5 percent higher than that of the natives. With a difference of 2 percent, the disparity is slightly smaller in the traditional states. The gap is smallest in moderate growth states, where the difference in labor force participation rates between natives and immigrants is less than one percentage point.

THE FOREIGN BORN ARE LESS LIKELY TO OWN A HOME

Homeownership rates are substantially lower among the foreign born than among natives. Table 1.7 shows the national homeownership rate for the native population is 72 percent, compared to 56 percent for the foreign born. The size of the gap varies. It is smaller in the traditional and moderate growth states but slightly larger the new settlement states, where the native homeownership rate of 73 percent is about 17 percent greater than the foreign-born rate. This likely reflects the shorter-than-average length of residency for immigrants in new settlement states. Over time it is possible that the foreign born in new settlement states will begin to purchase their own homes.

Table 1.6. Educational Levels of the Native and Foreign-Born U.S. Population, 2005

Traditional, New Settlement, and Moderate Growth States	Education: Less Than High School		Education: High School Graduates		Education: Some College, No Degree		Education: Associates Degree		Education: Undergraduate Degree		Education: Graduate, Professional	
	Native Born	Foreign Born	Native Born	Foreign Born	Native Born	Foreign Born	Native Born	Foreign Born	Native Born	Foreign Born	Native Born	Foreign Born
Total USA	**12.7%**	**31.4%**	**30.9%**	**22.9%**	**21.5%**	**12.8%**	**7.7%**	**5.9%**	**17.4%**	**16.0%**	**9.8%**	**11.1%**
Traditional States	12.3%	32.4%	28.5%	23.5%	24.4%	13.1%	7.5%	5.7%	17.4%	15.3%	9.8%	10.0%
New Settlement States	12.5%	27.2%	31.6%	23.3%	20.9%	13.2%	7.6%	5.9%	17.2%	16.5%	10.2%	13.9%
Moderate Growth States	12.6%	24.9%	32.1%	23.9%	21.6%	15.3%	8.1%	5.9%	16.8%	15.5%	8.8%	14.5%

Source: Same as Table 1.1.

Table 1.7.   Selected Educational and Economic Characteristics by Nativity and State

Traditional, New Settlement, and Moderate Growth States	Labor Force Participation Rate		Home Ownership Rate		150% of Official Poverty Line	
	Native Born	Foreign Born	Native Born	Foreign Born	Native Born	Foreign Born
Total USA	**65.7%**	**67.1%**	**71.6%**	**55.5%**	**21.1%**	**29.6%**
Traditional States						
California	64.6%	65.5%	63.5%	52.0%	20.4%	30.5%
Florida	60.4%	64.9%	72.3%	62.5%	21.2%	28.7%
Illinois	67.2%	69.0%	74.9%	64.5%	19.1%	24.2%
New Jersey	65.8%	68.4%	75.0%	55.6%	13.6%	20.1%
New York	63.6%	64.7%	64.4%	43.3%	20.4%	26.7%
Texas	66.6%	67.6%	69.1%	58.8%	26.2%	43.0%
Total	**64.7%**	**66.7%**	**69.9%**	**56.1%**	**20.1%**	**28.9%**
New Settlement States						
Alabama	61.4%	71.8%	72.9%	49.1%	27.7%	31.1%
Arizona	63.4%	67.5%	71.7%	57.1%	22.0%	39.3%
Arkansas	62.5%	71.9%	69.4%	52.6%	28.5%	46.7%
Colorado	71.3%	71.3%	72.7%	58.2%	17.5%	32.8%
Delaware	66.8%	70.8%	75.2%	50.7%	15.7%	25.8%
Georgia	67.0%	73.0%	70.0%	55.2%	23.2%	26.6%
Idaho	66.4%	68.2%	74.2%	51.7%	23.7%	40.2%
Indiana	66.8%	68.4%	75.9%	58.0%	19.8%	32.3%
Iowa	69.9%	70.7%	77.5%	62.5%	18.8%	31.3%
Kansas	70.4%	69.5%	73.9%	61.5%	19.7%	36.5%
Kentucky	61.6%	70.4%	73.7%	56.3%	27.3%	26.3%
Maryland	69.4%	72.9%	73.7%	62.2%	13.9%	16.9%
Minnesota	72.3%	71.3%	81.4%	57.3%	15.1%	31.5%
Mississippi	62.0%	75.8%	70.9%	57.8%	33.5%	33.1%
Missouri	66.5%	70.6%	73.9%	56.5%	22.1%	28.5%
Nebraska	71.4%	72.2%	73.4%	56.8%	18.9%	33.1%
Nevada	67.3%	68.9%	63.3%	58.9%	18.2%	25.6%
New Mexico	63.5%	66.2%	71.5%	59.5%	28.8%	46.1%
North Carolina	66.0%	72.9%	71.2%	49.9%	24.3%	36.5%
Oklahoma	63.6%	71.4%	70.2%	56.0%	27.1%	38.7%
Oregon	65.5%	67.7%	67.9%	51.7%	22.0%	38.7%
South Carolina	64.1%	71.0%	72.3%	50.3%	26.0%	34.6%
South Dakota	70.7%	67.4%	72.6%	45.2%	21.8%	37.4%
Tennessee	63.9%	71.4%	71.8%	54.4%	25.2%	31.0%
Utah	70.8%	70.5%	75.4%	59.2%	18.4%	34.1%
Virginia	67.5%	71.7%	73.1%	65.3%	16.4%	16.4%
Washington	66.8%	66.4%	69.5%	57.6%	18.6%	29.0%
Wisconsin	70.4%	65.2%	75.2%	54.1%	17.3%	32.1%
Total	**66.8%**	**70.3%**	**72.6%**	**55.9%**	**21.8%**	**32.6%**

(*continues*)

Traditional, New Settlement, and Moderate Growth States	Labor Force Participation Rate		Home Ownership Rate		150% of Official Poverty Line	
	Native Born	Foreign Born	Native Born	Foreign Born	Native Born	Foreign Born
Moderate Growth States						
Alaska	71.6%	72.6%	66.0%	69.3%	18.5%	16.2%
Connecticut	68.1%	70.2%	75.7%	60.2%	13.4%	16.8%
District of Columbia	66.3%	76.6%	45.8%	40.0%	27.4%	23.7%
Hawaii	65.3%	64.8%	64.0%	60.2%	14.9%	17.8%
Louisiana	62.3%	67.0%	70.6%	64.0%	30.0%	29.6%
Maine	66.7%	65.0%	75.4%	62.9%	20.8%	28.0%
Massachusetts	67.8%	68.3%	72.2%	51.7%	15.1%	21.9%
Michigan	65.6%	62.0%	78.5%	67.8%	20.6%	25.9%
Montana	68.0%	67.8%	70.9%	65.1%	25.1%	22.4%
New Hampshire	71.3%	68.8%	78.3%	62.4%	12.8%	18.2%
North Dakota	71.6%	73.7%	73.3%	45.4%	19.6%	26.2%
Ohio	66.2%	63.9%	73.8%	63.2%	20.9%	23.8%
Pennsylvania	63.9%	64.3%	76.3%	61.4%	19.6%	24.5%
Rhode Island	67.9%	68.0%	69.0%	52.2%	17.1%	28.5%
Vermont	71.4%	65.6%	74.8%	80.0%	18.9%	14.9%
West Virginia	55.3%	65.4%	77.1%	62.2%	28.9%	22.7%
Wyoming	71.6%	66.9%	74.3%	59.6%	16.7%	31.6%
Total	**67.1%**	**67.7%**	**71.5%**	**60.4%**	**20.0%**	**23.1%**

Source: Same as Table 1.1.

IMMIGRANTS ARE MORE LIKELY TO LIVE IN POVERTY THAN NATIVES

Table 1.7 shows the percentage of the population living below 150 percent of the poverty line—in other words, individuals who live in households with a total income less than 1.5 times the government-defined poverty cutoff point. Given that immigrants have less education and experience in the U.S. labor force, it is not surprising that immigrants are more likely than natives to live in poverty. The foreign born in new settlement states are more likely to live in poverty than their counterparts in both traditional states and moderate growth states.

This analysis of 1990, 2000, and 2005 data highlights the nature of the growth of the U.S. foreign-born population during the last 15 years. The immigrant population has grown over this time in states and regions with little prior exposure to the foreign born. Immigrants in the new settlement states are more likely to be newly arrived from abroad than in the traditional and moderate growth states. Thus, in comparison with the traditional and moderate growth states, the foreign-born population in the new settlement states tends to be younger with a proportionately higher number of recently arrived males. But otherwise new settlers do not greatly differ socio-economically from immigrants in established states. The greatest socio-economic differences tend to be not between immigrants in new and established areas, but rather between these states and the moderate growth states.

2

Integration Challenges
in New Settlement Areas

In spite of being a country largely shaped by immigration, the United States does not have immigrant policies. No federal laws explicitly promote cultural, economic or civic integration. Strategies and mechanisms facilitating immigrant integration emerged in the studied communities through trial and error, shaped by different variables in each community, including demographics and previous experiences with diversity. While governments of large immigrant receiving countries like Canada and Australia have implemented policies designed to bring immigrants into the fold, newcomers are not necessarily worse off in the United States.

Without officially endorsing multiculturalism, the U.S. government has developed a legal framework that nevertheless protects newcomers and guarantees a broad array of rights. Several policies protect both citizens and immigrants from discrimination on the basis of race, religion, nationality, and, in some cases, citizenship. These laws do not end prejudice, but they do provide solid footing for immigrants to defend their rights.

The private sector has also taken a role in promoting integration in the United States. Family members and employers sponsor immigrants and take a principal responsibility for ensuring their successful adaptation to their new country. A flexible labor market has facilitated the efforts of immigrant advocates by making employment easy to find. Although many jobs do not pay well, it is possible for immigrants to improve their lot and even own their own businesses. Given their high levels of employment, immigrants are frequently characterized as hardworking contributors to the nation's economy, which also eases the integration process.

Immigrant integration in the United States is aided indirectly by several broad and long-standing governmental policies. Among the most important

17

ones is birthright citizenship, granted automatically to children of immigrants born on U.S. territory. The provision applied even to the children of undocumented immigrants. As a result only one generation carries the label of "foreigner," in contrast, for example, to many European countries where third and fourth generations are still considered outsiders. Such policies reflect a deep-rooted national conviction that immigration is good for the country and immigrants are its future. The basic framework for naturalization dates back to the early nineteenth century and the ideas of the founding fathers that generally saw immigrants as presumptive citizens who should enjoy the same rights and privileges as other Americans.

While children of immigrants may be considered Americans from the day they are born, economic, cultural, and political integration takes place over a span of many generations. Like the children of immigrants who came decades ago, those who arrived in the most recent wave of migration see themselves as Americans and will almost certainly integrate more easily than their parents. However, that is not to say that they will achieve equal footing with their peers born to established residents. Integration does not happen overnight.

Time and overarching policy framework indirectly favor integration, but neither is a substitute for action at the community level, where the web of local relationships determines the immigrant experience. Indeed, one consequence of the federal government's hands-off approach to integration is an even greater reliance on community leadership. Experiences at local levels shape not only immigrant attitudes toward their new country but also the cohesiveness of the neighborhoods, towns, and cities they adopt as their new homes. Research in several new settlement communities indicates that local actors, including newcomers themselves, find novel ways to assume this responsibility and foster the incorporation of newly arrived immigrants into the broader society.[1]

The dynamics of integration, of course, cannot be reduced to negotiation between two groups. A categorization of two camps such as "established residents" and "newcomers" classifies individuals according only to when they arrived and does not account for infinite social divisions along ethnic, racial, and religious lines. The American host society itself is composed of different waves of newcomers, some more empathetic than others to the newest arrivals. Today's immigrant population is also comprised of several subcategories. Newcomers with refugee status benefit from generous U.S. assistance programs that can become a source of tension with other immigrants. In some cases, long-standing ethnic divisions are renewed in this country. This complexity means that immigrants arrive to find a country more diverse than the lands they leave behind. Integration becomes a multipronged process, with newcomers finding their way among the many segments of mainstream society and other immigrant communities.

Research in new settlement areas reveals many common obstacles to social, economic, and civic integration. While some of these challenges might be remedied with more effective policies, many of them also derive from cultural rifts that call for nothing less than changes in the perceptions that established residents, including earlier immigrants, and newcomers have of each other. Bridging the gaps that separate these different groups would strengthen communities; mitigate divisive social tensions; and position immigrants to participate more effectively in the wider society.

One obstacle is a perception among some established residents that new immigrants will leave as quickly as they came, thereby making it unnecessary to include them in broad society. The history of migrant workers in agricultural areas, for example, frequently conditions civic leaders to view immigrants as temporary residents. Even as Hispanics and other immigrants gain permanent employment, stereotypes of poor, wayward laborers remain prevalent in the public eye. In Virginia's Shenandoah Valley, the perception that immigrants comprised a transient workforce was transformed in some cases into a denial of responsibility for Hispanic health care, education, housing, and retirement needs.

The exclusion of immigrants from conceptions of local communities, beyond contributing to their marginalization, can also lead to depictions of newcomers as liabilities. Particularly amid economic difficulties, immigrants perceived as lacking links to a community are frequently accused of taking advantage of support networks, or, worse yet, taking jobs that would otherwise go to established residents. In Faribault, Minnesota, working-class Caucasians expressed fears that declines in local industries could make immigrants dependent on public assistance. African, Asian, and Latino immigrants were seen not as full-fledged members of the community, but rather temporary residents without reason to stay once their labor was no longer needed.

Progress in changing these deep-rooted notions is hindered by skewed perceptions of newcomers' legal status. Indeed, much of the opposition to migration stems from the widespread belief that the majority of foreigners in the United States are here illegally, even though the opposite is the case. At a national level, even when policymakers seek to restrict benefits for undocumented migrants, their decisions frequently affect family members who may be refugees or children who are U.S. citizens. At community levels, many programs and publications further complicate the issue by using definitions of immigrants that do not correspond with individuals' legal status. Examples include the designation of African-born children as "African Americans" in school data and counts of individuals who designate themselves "Latinos."

A common challenge is to emphasize the contributions made by newcomers, encouraging their acceptance as full-fledged members of the community and promoting tolerance. Whether focused on economic or social aspects, successful integration programs have generally helped established residents to acknowledge that immigrants bring something of value. Beyond labor, immigrant contributions highlighted by advocates included economic investment, cultural diversity, and the resuscitation of depopulated urban and rural areas. Responding to raising social tensions, the Atlanta suburb of Chamblee, Georgia, not only made public services more responsive to its newly diverse community but also took advantage of newcomers' economic and cultural activity to develop an "international village" with cross-cultural appeal. Elsewhere, however, the business community, while profiting from inexpensive labor force, has been notably absent from the public dialogue on immigration. In cases where police, school and health care representatives have depicted newcomers as a strain on community services, the business sector might stress that they also represent an irreplaceable resource.

By the same token, integration depends on the empowerment of immigrants for participation in a wider society. In both social and economic terms, it is important to stress opportunities and obligations as much as rights and entitlements. One of the largest obstacles to this goal is that mediating institutions—schools, hospitals, and local governments—often overlook the newcomer voice. This condition owes largely to immigrants' lack of familiarity with their new communities. Links of incorporation within newcomer groups and with broad society remedy this condition over time, but several smaller initiatives have potential to accelerate this orientation. Latino soccer tournaments organized in Salt Lake City, in one example, have encouraged players to identify with the communities represented by more than three hundred players.

Much as the benefits of immigration must be realized, integration also requires an honest and clear assessment of the problems faced by newcomers. To ignore the costs of immigration, including the fiscal costs to institutions unused to providing services to limited English proficient clients or the social costs when immigrants knowingly or inadvertently break laws or violate community norms, is to jeopardize the future integration of immigrants. The programs described in this handbook recognize such problems and seek solutions. Rather than hide domestic violence in immigrants families, The Immigrant and Refugee, Coalition Challenging Gender-Based Oppression aims to stop such abuse. Rather than ignore the costs that a lack of interpreters can inflict on immigrants and health services, several programs provide training and deploy bilingual personnel. Patching over such pitfalls as they emerge helps communities to avoid larger problems in the future.

Economically, opportunities for upward mobility represent a crucial incentive for newcomers to integrate themselves. Investment and professional advancement beyond ethnic businesses not only promote linkages with the host society but also help newcomers build foundations for their children. Whatever the level of integration, one pivotal task for new settlement areas is to ensure that newcomers are not disenfranchised. Low graduation rates among immigrant high school students reflect a failure of integration efforts to date. By limiting the number of bilingual role models in public schools, the trend also promotes a vicious cycle and increases the likelihood of greater challenges in the future. Initiatives such as the Dream Act, proposed by Senator Orrin Hatch of Utah, to make higher education more accessible to immigrants, represent promising top-down responses to such challenges.

For all the efforts by host communities to facilitate integration, newcomers take charge of their own lives in the United States soon after arrival. As they negotiate their own transition from newcomers to established residents, their success depends in part on the degree to which they coordinate their efforts with one another. Just like immigrants maximize their power vis-à-vis broader society by articulating common political and economic interests, they improve their own prospects in integration by asserting themselves with one voice. A united front is crucial particularly in states and localities where cultural or religious homogeneity marginalizes outsiders, but all newcomer communities benefit from coordinating the efforts of internal subgroups and advocates.

Such efforts allow newcomer groups to pursue their objectives more effectively, improve communication with the host society, and create political space that will benefit future generations.

NOTE

1. Elżbieta M. Goździak and Susan F. Martin, *Beyond the Gateway: Immigrants in a Changing America* (Lanham, MD: Lexington Books, 2005); and Victor Zuniga and Rueben Hernandez-Leon, eds., *New Destinations: Mexican Immigration in the United States* (New York: Russell Sage Foundation, 2005).

3

Communication Is Key: Enhancing English-Language Proficiency of Adult Immigrants

Knowledge of the English language is an important, if not the most important, measure of integration. While it is possible to find work without English language ability, language skills affect newcomers' capacity to earn sufficient wages to raise household income above poverty level. Participation in U.S. institutions and meaningful interaction with the mainstream community also rely greatly on language skills. Fluency in English correlates with upward mobility and attainment of economic, social, and cultural capital. Immigrants who are not able to communicate in English cannot represent themselves or benefit from a dialogue without the help of an interpreter. Communication barriers, in turn, often lead to tensions between newcomers and established residents. As Portes and Rumbaut write:

> In the United States, in particular, the pressure toward linguistic assimilation is all the greater because the country has few other elements on which to ground the sense of national identity. Made up of people coming from many different lands, lacking the unifying symbols of crown or millennial history, the common use of American English has come to acquire a singular importance as a binding tie across such a vast territory.[1]

Addressing language training needs of newcomers is therefore instrumental in fostering integration in all spheres of life. Immigration critics and community advocates alike cite lack of English language skills as a leading concern in many immigrant communities. According to the 2004 American Community Survey conducted by the U.S. Census Bureau, more than 80 percent of the foreign born speak a language other than English at home. Of this subgroup, 54 percent speak Spanish, 21 percent speak

Indo-European languages, 21 percent speak Asian and Pacific Islander languages, and four percent speak other languages. Among the foreign born who speak a language other than English at home, only 39 percent reported speaking English "very well," 25 percent "well," 24 percent "not well," and 13 percent "not at all."[2]

Research suggests that limited English skills cost businesses more than $175 million annually because of work-related miscommunication.[3] Poor English language skills also keep many immigrants in low-wage jobs.[4] Yet under existing immigration policies, there is no formal incentive for immigrants to learn English. The naturalization process requires applicants for U.S. citizenship to understand and speak a sample of short sentences. Critics point out that standards for passing the required English test seem arbitrary and do not reward those who actually learn the language.[5]

In 2004 more than 40 percent of the foreign born were naturalized.[6] The rate of naturalization among the foreign born continues to be a function of length of time spent in the country. Among those who arrived before 1970, 83 percent had obtained citizenship by 2002. Of those who entered the United States between 1970 and 1979, 73 percent had obtained citizenship by 2002, compared with 54 percent of those who entered between 1980 and 1989, 26 percent of those who entered between 1990 and 1999, and 5 percent of those entering after 2000.[7] Those that choose to maintain their permanent residency status and never naturalize face no English language requirement. And those immigrants that are undocumented and see no possibility of having their immigration status adjusted have even fewer incentives as well as opportunities to learn English. They live and work with co-ethnics speaking a common language; very few employers provide on-site English language classes.

Despite these deterrents, most immigrants recognize the value of learning English. According to the U.S. Department of Education, 1,172,569 adults were enrolled in federally funded English as a Second Language (ESL) programs in 2003–2004 alone.[8] This figure represents 43 percent of the overall enrollment in national adult education programs. English language skills open avenues to better paying jobs, increase opportunities to build social networks, and help ensure that immigrants will not be victimized by unscrupulous translators or others who might prey on their dependence.

Many newcomers and ethnic community leaders interviewed in the course of this study expressed interest in English language courses and advocated for improvement of ESL programs. But they also pointed out the many challenges that newcomers face in acquiring English language competency. Learning a new language is a challenge that most adults in the United States would find overwhelming. It can be even more difficult for adults with limited or no formal education in their native language. Immigrants who must work two or three jobs to make ends meet and immigrant women who work outside the home and care for small children face additional obstacles, particularly when language classes are held during the day or do not offer childcare. Nevertheless, learning English is essential in order to attain economic self-sufficiency and achieve social integration. Research has shown that participation in formal English language courses is important and more effective in the early stages of integration.[9]

English language training is now widely available to many immigrants. Almost every community has ESL training programs, but classes are frequently overcrowded with long waiting lists. In Seattle, a recent report counted three thousand adults on one program's waiting list, and more than one thousand immigrants were awaiting an opening in a New York public library program. In Dallas, there were reports of six thousand people on a one year waiting list. The quality of these programs also varies widely. Nevertheless, our fieldwork has identified shining examples of programs that have enhanced the English language competency of adults. There is no one formula. The model programs utilized a variety of funding strategies, involved different actors, followed different curricula, and were implemented at different venues.

DIVERSIFIED FUNDING IS CRUCIAL

Many English language program administrators indicated that long-term program sustainability rested on diversified funding sources. In cases of multiple funding sources, a loss of one funding stream did not necessarily spell disaster for the entire program. Many programs relied on federal funding, for seed money or as a long-term support, but private funding was also indispensable.

The revamping of the Adult ESL Program in Winchester, Virginia was made possible by a three-year 21st Century Grant from the U.S. Department of Education, while the *Horizonte* Instruction and Training Center, an alternative high school in Salt Lake City, Utah, has used grants from the federal Office of Refugee Resettlement (ORR) to educate refugees; other students pay nominal fees and/or seek scholarships to finalize their education. Several family literacy programs utilized Even Start or Head Start federal funding. Library-based programs, such as the ESL Conversation Club or the Multicultural Resources Center at the Glenwood Library in Greensboro, North Carolina, have used city funds and private donations as well as volunteer services to carry out their mission. In Greensboro, private donations are generated through the Greensboro Public Library Foundation, which was formed in 2002 to solicit support from individuals, businesses, civic groups, and foundations. Donors can choose from several giving plans: one-time donations, multiyear pledges, and estate gifts, gifts of appreciated stock for tax benefits and charitable remainder trusts or charitable gift annuities.

Imaginative use of resources, including use of volunteers, helps to keep overhead down and protect programs from funding interruptions. Almost every program examined in the course of our study took advantage of talented volunteers. At the Glenwood Library volunteers included both U.S.-born residents as well as immigrants. One of the immigrant volunteers, a retired native-speaker of Spanish, teaches Spanish to American library patrons. Another retiree, originally from France, facilitates discussions in the Conversation Club. Volunteers and mentors played a special role at *Horizonte* as well.

I have a Master's degree in English from the Sorbonne in Paris, France. I came to the United States a long time ago. I first came to the Conversation Club, because Lena, a student in my department, invited me to come. I'm a retired person, but I don't want to just stay at home all the time. I would like to do something to help foreign people to learn English, so I am very happy to be a member of the Conversation Club. My life goals are to stay in good health and to help people. By going to the Glenwood Library I stay active and get to help people in different ESL programs.

—Françoise Giraudet-Lay, France

CURRICULUM

When immigrants first come to the United States, they usually focus on gaining basic conversational skills in English to enable them to carry on face-to-face conversation in a social setting or at the workplace. However, with time many immigrants are also looking to gain or improve their proficiency in vocational language. We have heard employers indicate that lack of proficiency in vocational English is a major barrier to upward mobility. Several informants stressed that it is critical for ESL teachers to move beyond the functional English syllabus and to start providing a content-rich, high-standards curriculum that prepares ESL students to become academically successful in content learning. The Adult ESL Program director in Winchester, Virginia attributed the success of her program to the competency-based and level-based curriculum as well as block enrollment. In fact, most programs utilized a combination of competency-based and content-based curricula.

In many localities, English language programs combined language training with civic education or job skills training. This strategy helped participants gain skills necessary for long-term economic and social integration.

Horizonte structured the first block of English instruction around basic life and employment skills, including basic communication in specific areas (e.g., shopping, housing, transportation, etc.) and specific job skills (e.g., identification of career interests, resume writing, completion of job applications, etc.). Glenwood Public Library centered one of its English classes on training for the citizenship test. The International Institute of Minnesota established English for Work classes focused on basic language skills necessary to enter the workforce.

TAILORED DESIGN

The best English language programs would not have enjoyed such success if they did not take into account the particular characteristics and specific needs of the student population, in other words, if they were not custom-tailored. This student-focused, tailored approach produced programs that minimized access barriers.

Tailored program design requires accurate information about student populations to be served. Needs assessments can provide this information; they also encourage productive dialogue among participating groups. The Latino Connection in Winchester, Virginia conducted a needs assessment based on the Quaker Model of Compassionate Listening, discussed in more detail elsewhere in this handbook. The information obtained from the needs assessment indicated that the adult English as a Second Language infrastructure was in need of improvement. At the time of the needs assessment adult ESL classes were held at a variety of locations, including church basements, school cafeterias, and different workplaces, with no continuity from week to week. No mechanism was in place to group ESL students according to their language ability levels and class inscription was completely open. Beginner students shared classroom time with advanced students. Class sizes varied considerably, holding back the progress of adult ESL students at all levels. The needs assessment called for implementation of an ability-based curriculum with pre- and post-assessment testing that would allow students with different language skills to progress at their pace. Other needs identified in the course of the survey included: permanent locations for ESL classes, block enrollment, affordable rates, and free childcare during classes.

In order to minimize access barriers, several programs provided childcare, flexible class schedules, and low cost or financial assistance. *Horizonte* offers childcare on a first-come, first-serve basis through an on-site childcare center staffed with aides, volunteers, and peer parents. The International Institute of Minnesota attempted to accommodate students by offering its ESL classes either three afternoons or two evenings per week. Finally, several language programs were free-of-charge for certain categories of students (usually refugees, asylees or recent immigrants). Examples include *Horizonte*'s ESL program, the International Institute of Minnesota's English for Work Program, and the family literacy programs offered by the *Centro la Familia de Utah* and Even Start, both in Salt Lake City. The Glenwood Library was able to offer all its programs for free to the general public because of its wide base of city and community financial support.

Some recent immigrants are illiterate or functionally illiterate in their native language. Many programs take that into account in designing their English training programs and focus on literacy, including family literacy. For example, the *Centro la Familia de Utah* helps families develop language skills in both Spanish and English by teaching participants to record and share personal stories in both languages. The Even Start program provides English instruction to immigrant children and their parents. Family literacy programs also work to validate learners' cultures and languages of origin as part of English language training. The *Centro de la Familia de Utah* does this by using the knowledge already present in the family as a basis for instruction, while the Latin American Association has English and Spanish classes meet for an *intercambio* once a week that involves doing one activity completely in Spanish and one activity completely in English.

PUBLIC SCHOOL–BASED ADULT EDUCATION PROGRAMS

Adult ESL Program, Winchester, Virginia

In Winchester, Virginia, the Latino Connection, a coalition of local service providers and community advocates, worked with the Winchester City Public Schools, Literacy Volunteers of America, and the Shenandoah Valley Adult Education to improve and streamline Adult ESL programs. The TESOL (Teachers of English to Speakers of Other Languages) director at the Shenandoah University facilitated the process.

Using data from the previously mentioned needs assessment conducted by the coalition, ESL administrators were able to affect both enrollment and progress of adult students. Adult ESL classes used to be held in a variety of locations on an *ad hoc* basis, without any central supervision or standardized curriculum. Currently, the Winchester Public Schools (WPS) and the Northern Shenandoah Valley Adult Education (NSVAE) co-sponsor evening ESL classes held at a central location in the local middle school. There are four levels of instruction: new beginner, high beginner, intermediate, and advanced. The advanced level classes incorporate a civic education component. The curriculum is competency-based and regularly assessed, as is students' progress. Recently, block enrolment has been implemented to allow for further improvement. Childcare is provided to students with families.

The Latino Connection organized a Community Information Fair to publicize the new Adult ESL Program. The fair coincided with the opening of the Multicultural Resource Center that serves as a clearinghouse of information facilitating integration of newcomers to Winchester. The information campaign held at the fair covered a wide range of topics, including school enrollment, migrant education, and health care, nutrition, transportation, and support services. About 50–70 Latino community members attended, and *Winchester Star*, the local newspaper, covered the event.

As a result of the Adult ESL initiative spearheaded by the Latino Connection, student enrollment in adult ESL classes has increased to 370 students in Winchester alone. Furthermore, the competency-based and level-based curriculum, block enrollment, and high demand for the classes have lowered attrition rates.

All these efforts were initially supported by the 21st Century Grant, a three-year federal grant from the U.S. Department of Education, awarded to the Latino Connection and Winchester Public Schools. The aim of this grant is to provide academic enrichment and youth development to at-risk students as well as support community-based programs.

ALTERNATIVE HIGH SCHOOLS

At some alternative adult high schools, immigrants and refugees can complete their high school education and/or receive vocational training. *Horizonte* and Lincoln International School (previously Abraham Lincoln) are two examples of alternative high schools in Salt Lake City and Minneapolis, respectively.

Horizonte Instruction and Training Center, Salt Lake City, Utah

Our Students, Our Future

Horizonte Instruction and Training Center in Salt Lake City is designed to help students intellectually, culturally, and vocationally. One of four high schools in the Salt Lake City School District, *Horizonte* serves a diverse population; the school's 600 students range in age from twelve to eighty-five, come from 64 countries, and speak 82 languages. *Horizonte* offers six programs, including Alternative High School, Adult High School Completion, English as a Second Language, Young Parent, Directed Studies (flexible scheduling) and Applied Technology Center (trade instruction).

The primary focus of the ESL program is to provide intensive, survival and pre-employment English training.[10] The program includes 10 levels of instruction, ranging from preliterate, basic survival skills to postsecondary academic preparation and TOEFL (Teaching of English to Foreign Learners) training. The program runs year-round and includes five sessions, lasting approximately thirty-six days each during regular school year. There is also a summer term, lasting approximately twenty days from early June through early August.

Average class size is about 21 students, and volunteers from the University of Utah and other organizations help offset the teacher-student ratio and provide additional support in small group instruction. Teachers in both the day and evening programs have many years of experience in teaching ESL, and they hold both undergraduate and graduate degrees in that area.

The program adheres to an open-entry/open-exit policy. Registration and orientation for the day program is a mandatory three-day process that takes place weekly. Tests are administered to determine placement level. In order to set educational and career goals, past academic and work history is also recorded. A review of school policies and rules and a school tour are some of the other activities included in this registration/orientation session. Registration and orientation for entry into the evening program is a two-evening process that takes place at the beginning of each session (approximately every six weeks). In the day program classes are held from 8:30 am to 2:55 pm Monday to Friday. Night classes are held Tuesday, Wednesday, and Thursday from 6:00 to 9:00 pm.

There are eight periods of instruction in the day program. The first two periods make up one block class. This allows for more instructional time and less time spent in changing classes or other procedural tasks. The first, entitled "Life & Employment Skills," focuses on basic communication in specific areas (e.g., shopping, housing, transportation, etc.) and specific job related skills (e.g., identification of career interests, resume writing, completion of job applications, etc.). This block also includes a daily advisory component. The second block, entitled "Foundations of English," emphasizes more traditional, grammatical skills. Third and fourth period classes also combine to form the second block class. The two block classes have particular foci of instruction. Fifth period classes concentrate on reading skills. The remaining three classes focus on specific content areas including U.S. History, English Composition, Multicultural Studies, and Information Processing.

In 2003, *Horizonte* served 2,100 students in the day program and an additional 1,800 in the evening program. Students must be 18 years of age or older. The program serves legal residents, immigrants, and refugees. Those with a B-1 (Business) or B-2 (Tourist) visa are allowed to study part-time for a fee. American citizens and resident aliens pay a small fee for each 36-day session. Refugees are not charged because their fees are paid for by the Office of Refugee Resettlement (ORR). The fees for attending night classes are the same as those for the day program.

Recognizing the needs of students who are young parents or pregnant teens, *Horizonte* staffed an on-site childcare center with aides, volunteers, and peer parents. Childcare is offered on a first-come, first-served basis. In addition, an on-site office of the Department of Workforce Services, Career Fairs, Career Counseling, and other varied services help students better prepare for meaningful careers. Each student is assigned an advisor who works with students to attain their educational goals. These goals are, in almost every instance, linked to employment goals.

The initial assessment of past educational and work experiences, identified during the mandatory registration/orientation process, combined with ongoing monitoring of student goals and progress helps teachers design and implement specific learning activities that lead to both career attainment and career enhancement. Students are also encouraged to earn a U.S. high school diploma while enrolled. The program provides courses and counseling to help students accomplish this goal.

Technology skills obtained through the classes also help prepare students for life-long learning and career improvement. Students regularly engage in word processing and use multimedia presentation and employment-seeking software. They are also exposed to hardware items such as faxes, digital cameras, scanners and color laser printers.

Lincoln International High School, Twin Cities, Minnesota

Lincoln International High School (previously Abraham Lincoln High School) is operated by the non-profit Institute for New Americans with the goal of providing education and cultural opportunity to the Twin Cities' growing immigrant population. Lincoln is a Minneapolis Public Schools contract alternative high school. At the time of our research, the school had an enrollment of 315 students from 19 different countries who speak 29 different languages. Fifty-two percent of the students were non-Hispanic blacks (primarily from Africa), 44 percent were Hispanic (Mexico, Central America and South America), three percent Asian (Tibet and India), and one percent was U.S.-born. Ninety percent of the students were classified as "Limited English Proficient." On average, 85 percent of students attending four or more years go on to graduate; 80 percent of 2004 graduates are attending a two or four-year college or university.

Lincoln aims to provide a comfortable and safe environment where students can improve their English language skills and continue their adjustment to a new culture. The school bases its English immersion approach on the theory that people acquire fluency when they use the target language in their daily lives. English is therefore the primary language of instruction and communication, with bilingual support serving rather than supplanting that function. The English department curriculum includes classes in English grammar, reading/writing, and language art courses. Technology is used as appropriate in the classroom to reinforce critical concepts and skills. Students are required to complete eight semesters of core English credits in order to receive a high school diploma.

Through its Tutor/Mentor & Volunteer Program, Lincoln recruits, trains, and places community volunteers as tutors and mentors to help students develop English language skills, gain knowledge in basic subjects, and provides guidance for students in transition. This support is offered to students who want extra help to improve English language skills, build understanding of various subjects, receive homework help and complete general school assignments. Tutors are asked to give two to three hours of their time weekly and work one-on-one or with small groups of students. When tutors and students work particularly well together, mentoring relationships can be established and fostered for even greater support.

The volunteer program, comprised of community partnerships with St. Thomas University, the University of Minnesota, St. Mary's University and Breck School and over five hundred individuals from the community, supports the school's work. The volunteer program is funded by a grant from the federal government and coordinated by two staff members—one full-time and one half time—whose work is also supported by the grant. Those who wish to volunteer their time as tutors and mentors must complete a Volunteer Profile Form, and undergo both an interview process and a background check. Training and orientation is offered throughout the school year for program volunteers and activities are supervised within the facility to provide volunteers with any needed support.

PUBLIC LIBRARY-BASED PROGRAMS

Several libraries in the new settlement areas offered English language, family literacy, and citizenship programs for immigrants and refugees. In some localities these courses were very limited and relied on volunteers, while other sites had much more comprehensive programs. Below is a glimpse at two library-based programs: one offered at the Glenwood Library in Greensboro, North Carolina, the other in Hennepin County, Minnesota.

GLENWOOD LIBRARY, GREENSBORO, NORTH CAROLINA

The Glenwood Public Library in Greensboro, North Carolina responded to the area's new ethnic diversity by offering a wide range of English language, literacy, and citizenship programs for immigrants and refugees. All of these programs are housed in the Multicultural Resource Center, which hosts other citywide projects including the Hispanic Outreach and the Foreign Language Collection. The Foreign Language Collection includes materials in Arabic, Chinese, French, German, Hindi, Korean, Japanese, Russian, Spanish and Vietnamese.

The English for Speakers of Other Languages (ESOL) Program includes diverse language learning components. An English Conversation Club meets twice a week for approximately an hour and a half and provides opportunities for social networking. The Women's Literacy Class meets once a week and has beginning and intermediate levels. The library also offers training for tutors and publishes a quarterly ESOL newsletter, *Speak Out!*

Several classes are offered in partnership with teachers from a local community college. The Basic Reading and Writing Class is designed for individuals who have few or no reading and writing skills and meets twice a week for two hours. The more advanced TOEFL Preparation Class helps students prepare for the Test of English-as-a-Foreign Language. Finally, a Citizenship Class prepares participants for the citizenship interview and citizenship test and is held once a week for two and a half hours.

All programs offered through the library are free of charge. The City of Greensboro provides 90 percent of the Library's operating budget. Private donations are generated through the Greensboro Public Library Foundation, which was formed in 2002 to solicit support from individuals, businesses, civic groups and foundations. The purpose of the Foundation is to solicit additional financial assistance from non-governmental sources to enhance the facilities, services, book collection and other materials. Donors can choose from several giving plans including one-time donations, multiyear pledges, and estate gifts, gifts of appreciated stock for tax benefits and charitable remainder trusts or charitable gift annuities.

To supplement classroom learning, Glenwood Library hosts a large ESOL Collection including picture and bilingual dictionaries, audiovisual materials and materials related to grammar, TOEFL, U.S. citizenship, and general life skills. There is also an ESOL Computer Lab that provides self-paced and self-directed English learning programs. No computer experience is necessary to use the lab; a teacher (usually a volunteer) is always available to offer guidance and answer questions.

LIBROS Y MÁS AT THE
HENNEPIN COUNTY LIBRARY, MINNESOTA

In the last decade the Latino population has grown by over 200 percent in Hennepin County. In an effort to serve this growing population of potential library users, the Hennepin County Library developed a series of programs, initially based in two community libraries in the south suburbs, where large Latino communities reside. The goal was to facilitate access to library services for Latino families. The initial programs included computer classes, bilingual story time for children, and Spanish "Read to Me."

In early 2003, The Library Foundation of Hennepin County provided funding for a project called *Libros Y Más*. The idea was to put all Latino programming under one banner in order to increase the visibility of library programming for Latino families and increase the number of Latino library cardholders and readers. The project was planned, coordinated, and evaluated by a system-wide team, consisting of library staff from each of the library's five geographic areas and was co-chaired by the Library's Spanish Outreach Liaison and the Library's Programming Manager.

The team put together a resource packet and gathered information from key partners, such as South Hennepin Immigrant Services and the Hennepin County Office of Multicultural Services. Each participating library was asked to plan one or more programs in conjunction with a local partner that best met the needs of local Latino residents. Some libraries opted for cultural programming, such as storytelling and musical performances, others focused on skills such as computer classes. The programs were celebrated throughout Hispanic Heritage Month beginning in September 2003 and ended with a series of programs on *El día de los niños/El día de los libros* on April 30, 2004.

Libros Y Más resulted in over twenty new partnerships, a 40 percent increase in circulation of Spanish language materials, and an increase in the number of Spanish speakers with library cards. The most successful programs were those with the strongest partnerships. For example, one library teamed with ESL students from local elementary schools to create *Dia de los Muertos* (Day of the Dead) masks under the direction of a Mexican artist. The masks were then displayed in the library. Another library teamed with a Latino Arts high school in Minneapolis and hosted a similar exhibit. Another successful partnership involved teaming up with the Minneapolis Public Library to work with a Head Start program in a Latino neighborhood in south Minneapolis. The activities included an orientation session, bilingual story time, distribution of free books and puppets.

Latino adults participated in a number of computer literacy classes, conducted in Spanish. The classes ranged from four to six weeks and were geared toward adult learners. The curriculum included gaining familiarity with the Internet and e-mail, word processing skills, and use of online library catalogs. The course also focused on online resources such as the library's World Links and Job and Career Center.

FAMILY LITERACY PROGRAMS

Family literacy is a journey, not a destination

Centro de la Familia de Utah, South Salt Lake, Utah

Centro de la Familia de Utah is a private, non-profit organization founded in 1975 to address the unmet needs of the Latino community. Although the emphasis was originally on serving migrant and seasonal farm workers, over the years *Centro de la Familia* has developed expertise working with the entire family. Today, the center's mission is to strengthen the Latino family by promoting self-sufficiency through culturally competent social services. *Centro de la Familia* has chosen to focus on family literacy as the key to enhancing English language proficiency and literacy in both English and Spanish for Latino immigrant families.

The family literacy program is integrated into all Centro's programs that involve families. It fosters language skills in both Spanish and English and is based on the premise that parents—who are full of stories, regardless of their language skills—play a key role in nurturing a love of stories and books in their children. Instructors from the center help parents record and share their own stories as a starting point for cultivating literacy. As parents share their stories, they also share their culture, validating the knowledge already possessed by immigrant families. Building on their Spanish language skills, Latino parents learn to read and write in English more quickly and retain literacy in both languages. In 2004, the Family Literacy program gave away more than 1,200 books and sent home more than 2,300 literacy packets to help parents and their children develop literacy skills.

A key resource for participants is the Américas Award Reference and Resource Library, a collection of fiction, poetry, folklore and non-fiction for children and young adults, published in Spanish and English. Américas literature ranges from picture books for children to mature works for young adults. As immigrant families enrolled in the program share stories found in this collection, they develop their reading skills and enhance their cross-cultural communication skills.

Centro de la Familia receives public funds through the Migrant Head Start Program and is able to serve migrant families who derive most of their income from agricultural work. Support also comes from private donations, including corporations, foundations and individuals. Current donors include Bank One, the Wal-Mart Foundation, the Qwest Foundation as well as many local businesses.

Even Start Family Literacy Program, Salt Lake City, Utah

The Even Start Family Literacy program, hosted by Salt Lake City's Western Hills Elementary School is a need-based program with participant eligibility established under the Head Start Act.[11] Even Start is an educational program for the nation's low-income families that is designed to improve the academic achievement of young children and their parents, especially in the area of reading. Even Start combines four core components, which make up family literacy: 1) early childhood education; 2) adult literacy (adult basic and secondary-level education and/or instruction for English language learners); 3) parenting education; and 4) interactive literacy activities between parents and their children.

The director of the Western Hills program is its only full-time employee. In an interview, he described a situation where funding for the program is diminishing even though needs increase. In addition to recent cuts to the federal Even Start budget, the program is also affected by its location in an unincorporated part of the county. This area attracts immigrant families because housing is less expensive, but at the same time location in an unincorporated area means that access to funds for integration activities is limited.

Waiting lists for the program are consistently long. In 2003–2004, the program served approximately 45 families and maintained 60–70 families on the waiting list. In the summer of 2005, over 100 families were on the list. In order to keep the program alive for those it *can* serve, the program director has applied for private grants to cover funding shortfalls—a very time-consuming process. Eligibility for the program has also been limited to children under six years of age. The director would like to make the program more convenient by providing evening classes; however, that would entail accepting older siblings of current participants, which is impossible under current budget constraints. Finally, volunteers are often employed in place of paid teachers. Using volunteers helps the bottom line, but entails additional management tasks associated with locating, scheduling and motivating volunteers.

The Even Start Family Literacy Program is free to qualifying participants. Even Start was first authorized by the federal government in 1988 with an appropriation of $14.8 million. The program became state-administered in 1992 when the appropriation exceeded $50 million. Most recently, the program was reauthorized by the Literacy Involves Families Together Act of 2000 and the No Child Left Behind Act of 2001. Even Start allocations in fiscal year 2004 for all states totaled $246,910,000.

ETHNIC COMMUNITY ASSOCIATION-BASED PROGRAMS

Latin American Association, Atlanta, Georgia

English language instruction is often provided by larger organizations that serve a particular immigrant population. In Atlanta, The Latin American Association (LAA) provides a broad range of services to its members.[12] The services of the LAA are developed in response to the Latino community's needs and include: English language/literacy instruction, legal aid, pre-employment skills training, job-placement, youth mentoring program, youth internship program, homeownership program, and other social services. In 2004, LAA assisted more than 60,000 individuals and their families.

LAA is funded through grants and donations from more than 80 businesses and foundations. In 2004, contributors included the Coca-Cola Company, the UPS Foundation, the Fannie Mae Foundation, State Farm Insurance Companies, Cingular Wireless and the Atlanta Journal-Constitution. The significant support from these organizations is supplemented with monetary or in-kind contributions from individuals.

The LAA's English as a Second Language program teaches adults who are not English proficient to understand the English language and to learn how to use English in different contexts. The goal is to help individuals reach their maximum potential. ESL classes are offered at LAA's main office and at employer locations around the Atlanta region. The ESL program at LAA is based on the idea that students must be active participants in their learning and work together cooperatively to successfully acquire the target language.

The instruction focuses on learners' strengths and on real communication and life skills. Learners work in pairs and small groups, as well as individually, and courses integrate all skills: reading, writing, speaking, and listening. Once a week, each English class meets with its sister Spanish class for an *intercambio*. This involves doing one activity completely in Spanish and one activity completely in English. The *intercambio* provides a unique opportunity for students to practice and reinforce their newly acquired language skills with native speakers of the target language. In 2004, LAA provided language education services to 1,575 individuals. Classes are fee based.

The LAA also offers on-site English classes for employers in the metro Atlanta area. Customized language programs are available in a wide variety of fields including legal, mortgage, financial, customer service, real estate, medical, human resources, social services, and manufacturing.

SOCIAL SERVICE AGENCY-BASED ESL PROGRAMS

International Institute of Minnesota, St. Paul, Minnesota

The International Institute of Minnesota is a non-political, non-sectarian social service agency founded in 1919 to serve both foreign- and native-born. It is affiliated with the U.S. Committee for Refugees and Immigrants (USCRI) and the United Way. The mission of the Institute is to: 1) provide a center for information and assembly for all nationalities and races; 2) develop fellowship and understanding among such persons through group meetings and activities; 3) promote the welfare of the foreign born and their families; and 4) preserve and stimulate intercultural values. Program areas include casework and refugee resettlement, education (employment training, language learning and citizenship), and intercultural relations.

The International Institute offers ESL classes to adults whose native language is not English and who need to improve basic skills in speaking, listening, reading, writing, or grammar. Classes are very diverse, with a range of cultural, educational, and professional backgrounds represented. A comprehensive curriculum is used to help students progress from a beginning to an advanced level, as well as chart their English language acquisition. Certificates of Attendance are awarded to students and Certificates of Completion can be requested.

Classes are offered at beginning through advanced levels. All new students must have an interview and take an entrance exam to determine proper level of entry. Test dates are scheduled two weeks before each session. Sessions lasting ten weeks are offered beginning in January, March, June and September. ESL classes are offered three afternoons or two evenings a week, and advanced learners can opt for a conversation class that meets twice a week.

English for Work (EFW) classes are offered to refugees, immigrants and asylees. These intensive classes address the needs of refugees and immigrants who must learn English as quickly as possible in order to enter the workforce. Up to 20 hours of classes are offered for pre-literate through advanced-level students that address both language and cultural skills. The topics covered are relevant to their daily lives. Students improve their language and employment skills while also learning practical tools for functioning in their communities. The classes prepare students to use language and cultural skills to fulfill daily responsibilities in the home and workplace, find and retain employment, communicate effectively with co-workers, supervisors, police, health care providers, and customer service agents, understand and complete forms needed in the workplace, and develop basic computer skills. Strategies include using role plays to practice language and work skills and field trips that have an employment and/or community-related focus.

Students are divided into two groups based on level of English language ability. Refugees at the beginner through intermediate levels are eligible to attend the EFW Language Class, focused on intensive English language training, including grammar, reading, writing, conversation and listening skills. Sixteen hours per week are spent in the classroom (including one hour of computer lab). Intermediate through advanced level refugee, asylee and immigrant students are eligible for the EFW Communication and Computer Class. This class combines English language and civics instruction with computer literacy, including introduction to word processing, internet job-search, and resume preparation. Instruction includes seven hours of classroom work and seven hours in the lab. Entering students are evaluated using the Comprehensive Adult Student Assessment Systems (CASAS) English Placement Test prior to the enrollment and at the end of each session to monitor progress. Enrollment is based on slot availability.

ESL classes are fee-based. English for Work classes are funded by the federal Office of Refugee Resettlement and are free to qualifying individuals.

NOTES

1. Alejandro Portes and Rubén G. Rumbaut, *Legacies: The Story of the Immigrant Second Generation* (Berkeley: University of California Press, 2001), 114.

2. U.S. Census Bureau, American Community Survey 2004, Public Use Microdata.

3. Little Hoover Commission, *We the People: Helping Newcomers Become Californians* (Sacramento, CA: Little Hoover Commission, June 2002).

4. National Center for Policy Analysis, *Immigration: Language Barrier Problems*. www.ncpa.org/pd/immigration/pidmm/pidmm6.html (September 24, 2006).

5. Jane Eisner, "Discretion Can Be Better Part of Citizenship," *Holland Sentinel*, 25 January, 2001.

6. U.S. Census Bureau, American Community Survey 2004.

7. U.S. Census Bureau, American Community Survey 2004.

8. U.S. Department of Education, Office of Vocational and Adult Education, "Enrollment and Participation in the State-Administered Adult Education Program: Total Enrollment by ABE, ESL and ASE Levels." http://www.ed.gov/about/offices/list/ovae/pi/AdultEd/aedatatables.html (November 14, 2005).

9. N.V. Hanh, "Southeast Asian Refugee Resettlement in the United States: A Socioeconomic Analysis," in *American Mosaic: Selected Readings on America's Multicultural Heritage*, ed. Y.I. Song and E.C. Kim (Englewood Cliffs, NJ: Prentice Hall, 1993).

10. http://www.slc.k12.ut.us/sites/horizonte/

11. Family income must be less than 125% of poverty level.

12. For more information see: www.latinamericanasoc.org.

4

Addressing Economic Needs: Vocational Training, Re-Credentialing, and Micro-Enterprise

English language competency is not the only factor that facilitates immigrant integration. Many newcomers, even those who speak English, benefit from access to vocational training and re-credentialing. According to the U.S. Census Bureau, immigrants aged 25 or older were less likely to have graduated from high school than natives the same age: 67.2 percent and 87.5 percent, respectively. More than one-fifth of the foreign born had less than a ninth-grade education (21.5 percent), a higher proportion than that of the native population (4.1 percent).[1]

The highest percentages of high school graduates among the foreign born were from Asia (87.4 percent) and Europe (84.9 percent). In contrast, the percentage of high school graduates from Latin America was much lower (49.1 percent), and Central Americans were the least likely to have high school diplomas (37.7 percent). The proportion of those with a bachelor's degree ranged from 50.0 percent for Asians to 11.6 percent for Latin Americans.[2] These statistics clearly indicate that Latin American immigrants are most in need of educational services, including vocational training.

A recent study by the Urban Institute reported among its key findings:

- Immigrants are 11 percent of all U.S. residents, but 14 percent of all workers and 20 percent of low-wage workers.
- Immigrants' hourly wages are lower on average than those for natives, and nearly half earn less than 200 percent of the minimum wage—versus one-third of native workers.
- Immigrant workers are much more likely than natives to drop out of high school (30 percent versus 8 percent), and are far more likely to have less than a ninth-grade education (18 versus 1 percent).

- Three-fourths of all U.S. workers with less than a ninth-grade education are immigrants.
- Nearly two-thirds of low-wage immigrant workers do not speak English
  proficiently, and most of these workers have had little formal education.[3]

These statistics speak to the clear need to improve employment prospects
of immigrant workers. They also point to the interdependent nature of
English language acquisition, educational attainment, and vocational
training. The increasing prominence of Vocational English as a Second
Language (VESL) programs demonstrates recognition that English language training cannot be separated from vocational training among workers with limited English language proficiency.

There were several promising vocational training programs in the studied
new settlement sites, including a variety of programs training health care
workers; a training program focused on newcomers with background in
farming; and micro-enterprise training programs.

Successful vocational programs carefully researched both the supply of
local labor force and the demand of local labor markets. For example, the
Farm Incubator/Immigrant Farming Project offered through the University
of Minnesota Outreach, Research and Education Park, caters to immigrants
with background in farming and trains them to farm small plots of land
using modern farming methods and sell their products at local farmers'
markets for several years, until the trainees are ready to purchase or lease
their own land. The growing demand for organically grown produce in the
Twin Cities ensures a robust market for the fruits and vegetables grown by
immigrant farmers.

An example of a program which took into consideration both work experiences of refugee newcomers and the demands of the local labor market is
the Refugee Healthcare and Medical Mentorship Project (RHEMP), run by the
Lutheran Services of Georgia. The immediate impetus to launch the training
program was a decision by the nearby DeKalb Medical Center to build a $67
million hospital. The medical center foresees a need for a multicultural, multilingual staff to attend to the increasingly diverse community in the Atlanta
area. The goal of some micro-enterprise training programs was not only to
promote economic integration of immigrants by equipping them with skills
necessary to establish fiscally viable businesses, but by doing so revitalize
whole immigrant neighborhoods or depressed commercial areas. This approach benefited both the immigrants and the larger community.

TRAINING HEALTH CARE WORKERS

The aging of the U.S. society is generating an increased demand for all
types of health care workers, including specialized geriatric physicians and

nurses in hospitals, health care providers in assisted living and nursing homes as well as in-home service providers for the elderly. The U.S.-born labor force is unable to meet this demand, which creates an unprecedented opportunity for immigrants interested in employment in the health care systems. Training or re-credentialing immigrants for these positions thus represents a sound and logical approach to ameliorating the health care worker shortage.

Faced with a shortage of nurses, the International Institute of Minnesota has developed career-training programs funded by the United Way, the State Refugee Coordinator's office, the federal Office of Refugee Resettlement (ORR), and the McKnight Foundation. In Atlanta, Georgia, a decision by the DeKalb Medical Center to build a $67 million hospital was an impetus for the Lutheran Services of Georgia to launch a training program for refugees and immigrants with work experience in the health care field to re-enter their profession in the United States. See detailed discussion of these programs in the chapter on facilitating immigrants' access to culturally sensitive and linguistically appropriate health care.

VOCATIONAL TRAINING FOR FARMERS

In many localities immigrant and refugee farmers had few employment skills transferable to the U.S. labor market. Both North Carolina and Minnesota have sizable refugee populations with background in traditional farming. There are about ten thousand Hmong residing in North Carolina; most of them arrived in the state as secondary migrants from other areas in the United States. North Carolina is also home to approximately 1,600 Montagnards. Both groups have been farmers in their countries of origin. Similarly Minnesota; the state is home to large number of refugees from Vietnam and Laos, along with Hmong from several countries in Southeast Asia. Many of them were slash-and-burn farmers and make excellent candidates for training programs in agriculture.

Farm Incubator Program and New Immigrant Farming Project, Rosemount, Minnesota

The Farming Incubator Program (FIP) provides hands-on and classroom-based agricultural training for new immigrant and beginner farmers at the University of Minnesota Outreach, Research and Education Park (UMore) in Rosemount, MN. Trainees participate in the education program for three years and are allowed to farm one to three acres. The primary objectives of the program are: to teach food production jointly with farm management and business planning, give new farmers an opportunity to refine growing techniques, and enable new farmers to build equity so they can purchase land when they graduate. Participants sell their produce at local farmers' markets. Graduating trainees are expected to transition from UMore Park facility to parcels of land leased or purchased. Trainees pay minimal fees to enroll in the program.

The New Immigrant Farm Program (NIFP), active since 1999, helps new immigrant farmers increase their farm-level productivity, profitability, and sustainability. Families may farm one to three acres on University property, or may use their own land. Similarly to the incubator program, the new immigrant farm training lasts three years and provides students with knowledge of vegetable production, soil fertility management, alternative crops, pest control, post harvest handling, processing, marketing, farm management, and record keeping. The program offers training materials in English, Hmong and Spanish on essential farming topics. About 85 percent of the program's current participants are Hmong, and the remaining participants are from East Africa, Europe and Central America.

Farming training programs can have broad impact: "The benefits of farming go beyond money, according to Nigatu Tadesse, a former extension educator and assistant professor who coordinated the NIFP. 'For new immigrants, farming is engraved in their culture,' he says, 'and sometimes it is therapeutic.' As Tadesse explains, farming is a way of life for many families, a link to culturally important foods that are not available in mainstream grocery stores. Growing one's own food provides the opportunity to be one's own boss, become an entrepreneur and gain greater independence."[4]

MICRO-ENTERPRISE TRAINING PROGRAMS

Neighborhood Development Center, St. Paul, Minnesota

Neighborhood Development Center, Inc. (NDC) is a community-based non-profit organization that works in low-income communities of Twin Cities and surrounding suburbs. NDC assists emerging entrepreneurs to develop successful businesses that provide them with meaningful employment and source of income as well as enhance economic development of their communities. NDC assists communities in local job creation, generating local income and wealth, strengthening the local economy, creating community leaders, creating visible signs of redevelopment, and creating businesses that will serve as community gathering places. NDC employs neighborhood development, micro-enterprise and community organizing strategies to reach its goals.

NDC has adapted to changing needs throughout its development. At its start in 1993, NDC provided only business training. Then, in 1994, NDC expanded its services to include affordable financing options. In subsequent years, NDC added other services, including technical assistance in 1996, business incubation beginning in 1997, and real estate development services starting in 2002. Currently, NDC partners with 18 neighborhood and ethnic community-based organizations to provide entrepreneur training, financing, ongoing support and real estate services in the low-income neighborhoods of Minneapolis and St. Paul, serving in five distinct ethnic groups: African Americans, Native Africans, Hmong, American Indians and Latinos. NDC receives funding from both public and private sources. NDC funders from 2003 to 2005 included the Office of Refugee Resettlement, the Cities of St. Paul and Minneapolis, the Small Business Administration, American Express and the Ford Foundation.

The Micro Entrepreneur Training Program is a 16-week course offered twice a year (in spring and fall cycles) in each community NDC serves. The training course consists of eight classroom sessions, and eight one-on-one sessions of individualized training and technical assistance. Classes are taught by professional small-business training consultants, and cover the fundamentals and techniques of marketing, operations, financial management and writing a solid business plan.

Since 1993, NDC has trained over 2,300 entrepreneurs to start or expand their existing businesses. As a result of the Entrepreneur Training Program, over 600 businesses started or were strengthened. Graduates of the NDC training program are eligible to participate in business-development activities at Mercado Central, a retail center made up of more than thirty small Latino businesses.

NDC provides scholarships for low- to moderate-income individuals. In order to qualify for a scholarship, participants must meet income guidelines and live in one of NDC's targeted neighborhoods.

NOTES

1. Larsen, Luke J. 2004. "The Foreign-Born Population in the United States: 2003." Current Population Reports, P20–551, U.S. Census Bureau, Washington, DC.

2. Larsen, "The Foreign-Born Population."

3. Randy Capps, et al., "A Profile of the Low-Wage Immigrant Workforce," Immigrant Families and Workers Brief No. 4, Urban Institute, 2003.

4. Devon Idstrom, "Community Dividend," August 1, 2003.
http://minneapolisfed.org/pubs/cd/03-1/farmers.cfm (August 27, 2004).

5

Dreaming about Education:
Enhancing Educational
Opportunities for
Immigrant Children

High levels of immigration in the 1990s have led to a rapid increase in the number of children in immigrant families. In 2000, immigrants represented one in nine of all U.S. residents, but their children represented one in five of all children less than 18 years old. About three-quarters of children of immigrants are U.S.-born, while about one-quarter are foreign-born. The share of children of immigrants among the school-age population has also grown rapidly, from 6 percent in 1970 to 19 percent in 2000. In 2000 there were 11 million children of immigrants enrolled in pre-K through 12th grade out of 58 million school children.

The share of first-generation immigrant children increases in the upper grades. In 2000, 16 percent of all children in pre-kindergarten were children of immigrant parents, but only 2 percent were foreign born. In the middle and high school (6th to 12th grade), children of immigrants accounted for 19 percent of the total student population, while the foreign born represented 7 percent of the total. In the upper grades, over one-third of all children of immigrants were first-generation, compared with only one-eighth in pre-kindergarten.[1]

THE EDUCATIONAL NEEDS OF
NEW NORTH CAROLINIAN CHILDREN

Indeed, public school systems in the new settlement areas studied in the course of our research were the first arenas where the impact of recent newcomers was felt the most. Siler City in North Carolina reported in 1997 that close to 50 percent of the kindergarten children were native Spanish speakers.[2]

Similar growth occurred in parts of Georgia. Close to 13 percent of the students enrolled in the public school system of DeKalb County, Georgia, in the 2001/2002 school year were categorized as "international students" (i.e., foreign-born students or U.S.-born children of immigrant parents). At the time of our study, the county had 83 public elementary schools, with an average enrollment of 581 students. The enrollment of students in immigrant families exceeded one hundred in 19 of these schools, where students in immigrant families ranged from 21 percent to a high of 85 percent of the total student population. In seven of these schools students in immigrant families constituted the majority of the student population, while 24 schools had fewer than ten international students and in 15 others international students comprised one percent or less of the student body.[3]

The unprecedented growth of students in immigrant families has posed numerous challenges to the school systems in new settlement sites examined in the course of this study in terms of their ability to provide high quality education to newcomer students, including their ability to enhance students' English language proficiency. Researchers have noted that one cause of the challenges in the nation's English as a Second Language (ESL) or Teaching English to Speakers of Other Languages (TESOL) programs is that administrators have not adapted to changing trends among the non-English speaking community. For example, the *Washington Post* reported that in 2002 Montgomery County School District in Maryland still used an ESL program "designed decades ago primarily for well-educated Cubans fleeing Fidel Castro's regime." Because of such outdated programs, less privileged immigrant children, representing hundreds of different languages and countries may be at a disadvantage. Analysts also believe that the nation's ESL programs may not be improving because, until recently, such programs have been low on most schools' lists of priorities. Patricia O'Neill, Vice President of the Montgomery County School Board, explains that no one has taken the initiative to reform the ESL system in her area because, as she puts it, "It's been nobody's baby."[4]

The North Carolina public school system did not have designated English for Speakers of Other Languages (ESOL) curriculum and did not require EASOL certification to teach English to Limited English Proficient (LEP) students. While there were many committed and qualified teachers in the local school system, most ESOL teachers in the Triad transferred from other fields. Without an educational infrastructure to advocate for improved standards, internal advocacy came primarily from committed ESOL instructors, teachers who struggled to reach their foreign-born students, and administrators who did not want their schools to be penalized for poor standardized test results.

A chronic problem in North Carolina public schools and other new settlement sites was the disenfranchisement of immigrant youth. School enrollment of Hispanic students dropped sharply in North Carolina at age six-teen, when the state no longer requires attendance. The fact that Hispanic youth leave school as soon as legally possible indicates that they do not feel engaged in the learning process. The influx of Hispanics in North Carolina has been so sudden that few members of the ethnic community have had time to advance their education and establish themselves as bilingual role models. Educators have sought to address the drop in enrollment but with-out significant success. Less is known about dropout rates among other im-migrants residing in North Carolina. It is possible that ethnic leadership in-terventions, congregational involvement, and influential mentors have reduced dropout rates among refugee youth. Another likely scenario is that children's success in school is directly related to the educational level of their parents. Anecdotal evidence suggests that children of Montagnard and Cambodian farmers are less likely to complete school than children of Bosnian technicians or African educators.

Immigrant children in Guilford County face many obstacles to educa-tional achievement. In the summer of 2002, the county school system elim-inated designated magnet schools and related programs for ESOL students. Children were assigned to neighborhood schools with minimal ESOL re-sources. Cynics believed that the decision was made to artificially raise school test scores because "special populations" of fewer than 20 students enrolled in a U.S. school for less than two years can be excluded from test score calculations.

In response to an outcry among immigrant advocates and educators, an immigrant advocacy group in Guilford County began researching the sit-uation. The Multicultural Advisory Council interviewed parents and teach-ers of Limited English Proficient (LEP) students and consulted the federal office of Civil Rights to ascertain whether children's civil rights were vio-lated. The school administration invited a national team of consultants to review the school system's approach to LEP learners and their families. The Council of Great Cities Schools (an organization of eighty of the largest school districts in the nation) sent a team of consultants to Greens-boro in fall 2002 to review the situation. Their assessment and recom-mendations for serving LEP students, *Beyond Proficiency: Creating a State-of-the-Art Multilingual Program* was being reviewed by the Guilford County School System at the time of the study. Among the recommendations was a call to ensure immigrant community representation and input in the school decision-making process. At the time of this writing, incremental changes did take place. For example, a new position of an ESOL director had been created when immigrant parents voiced their concerns that there was no oversight of ESOL language training. Currently 34 public schools provide ESOL instruction for approximately 2,400 LEP students. These students come from 85 countries and speak 75 primary languages. There appears to be a plan to consolidate these children in fewer schools to maximize resources and enhance support for LEP students. Some community leaders believe that these proposed plans are a direct result of the needs assessment, but nobody wanted to speak to these issues on the record.

THE GLEN HAVEN TUTORIAL CENTER, GREENSBORO, NORTH CAROLINA

To make up for the deficiencies of the public school system several agencies serving immigrant communities collaborated to establish the Glen Haven Tutorial Center. In January 2004, under the leadership of the Center for New North Carolinians (CNNC), Lutheran Family Services, Centro de Accíon Latino, Faith Action International, and African Services Coalition created an after-school tutorial program for the children (kindergarten through high school) who live in the Glen Haven Apartment Complex. The tutorial program is open Monday to Thursday from 2:45 to 5:30. "Fun Friday" is every Friday. The Tutorial Center is staffed by volunteers and social work student interns. The Coordinator of the Tutorial Center is a retired professor of social work from High Point University, who currently serves as AmeriCorps member with CNNC.

The apartment complex houses numerous Montagnard families plus a moderate number of Latino, Liberian, and African-American families. A teacher from Jesse Wharton School summed up the success of the project during a recent visit to the tutoring center: "Now we know why these children are doing so well in school; it's because they have help with their homework here at the Tutorial Center."

THE WINCHESTER PUBLIC SCHOOL ESL PROGRAM, VIRGINIA

My goal is to end the cycle of having the LEP students in ESL classes all day only to be let out for art and physical education classes.

We are now focusing on providing a content based ESL program that will facilitate the transition from ESL to mainstream classes for the non-native English speakers.

The Winchester Public School (WPS) system, on the other hand, has had better success in adapting to the demographic changes of the community it serves. The number of ESL students in the WPS has increased over 750 percent since the 1996/1997 school year.

Currently, the English-as-a-Second Language program serves approximately 500 students in grades K–12. The program emphasizes both English language proficiency and core area academics. Students in the elementary grades receive instruction in both regular and ESL classrooms. At the secondary level, the program is offered according to the students' level of English language proficiency.

Until the 2001/2002 school year, the ESL program of the WPS was run autonomously at each designated site of instruction. Oral proficiency was the focus of the curriculum, with much less emphasis on reading and writing. Currently, ESL instruction in the WPS embraces an integrated, research-based literacy model that focuses on building oral and written fluency, comprehension, and vocabulary from the very beginning an ESL student enters the school system. The impetus for implementing this particular model of ESL instruction was to break the cycle of Limited English Proficient (LEP) students spending the entire day in ESL classes, with a break only for art and physical education.

To facilitate the registration process for students, the Winchester Public Schools ESL Intake Center opened in April 2005. The center functions as the system-wide registration and assessment site for all incoming students and serves as a resource center for ESL families. Staff members help parents to complete registration paperwork, and assess the English language proficiency levels of new students.

ESL students enrolled in the Winchester school system repeatedly expressed a desire to move into a mainstream course of study. Oscar, a 15-year old student, enthusiastically showed us numerous works of art, some featured on local TV, which he created during the five years since his migrant family settled in Winchester. Despite a demonstrated artistic talent and verbal articulation of interest in art, Oscar longingly spoke of his desire to take the same academic classes as the mainstream students. His younger sister also admitted to being bored in the ESL classes and was anxious to make friends with a wider circle of students at her elementary school. The major overhaul of the ESL program at the WPS is a clear indication that the school administration would like to make Oscar's dreams the reality for all ESL students.

MIGRANT EDUCATION TOWARD ACADEMIC SUCCESS, VIRGINIA

High school students in the Shenandoah Valley who want to pursue higher education find a lot of support from the Migrant Education Toward Academic Success (METAS) program run by the local Migrant Education Program.

METAS offers monthly informational sessions on a wide array of topics related to higher education and career development as well as individual mentoring and support for its participants. A big question for Latino migrants who are considering going to college is how to pay for higher education. Most of the students' parents work in low paying jobs and have large families; the students know that they cannot rely on parents to provide much financial support for their college education. While we were conducting this research, METAS organized an information session about the different options of financing college education. Migrant student advocates who ran the information session shared their own strategies, including work-study programs, working part-time while attending college, and applying for financial aid and student loans. Migrant students applied this information in a Scholarship Scavenger Hunt designed to hone their financial application skills and sustain their motivation to purse higher education.

In the spring of 2004, in an attempt to reciprocate the students' hospitality and willingness to talk to the research team, we had invited a group of twelve students to visit Georgetown University. The students went on a guided-tour of Georgetown's campus, participated in an orientation session, which included information on financial aid and on campus housing, and ate lunch in one of the student dining halls. One student, an aspiring artist, had a chance to show his portfolio to one of the art professors and received encouragement as well as practical advice on how to pursue his artistic dreams. The daylong trip to Washington, DC, included sightseeing and museum hopping. At the Museum of American History, the students toured an exhibition entitled *Our Journeys, Our Stories: Portraits of Latino Achievements*, which featured portraits and bilingual biographies of 25 distinguished Latinos. After a walk around the Jefferson Monument, the trip concluded with a dinner at a local Salvadoran restaurant.

The Shenandoah Valley has a long history of providing services to migrant workers and their children. A comprehensive support service network for migrant farm workers has developed over the past two decades and many committed individuals continue to advocate on behalf of children in immigrant families. Despite tireless efforts of many advocates, Virginia's House of Delegates subcommittee effectively killed for the year a bill that would have allowed some undocumented migrant children access to in-state tuition rates at Virginia colleges and universities. The committee heard testimony from Leo Alonso, a Blue Ridge Community College student who moved to the United States from Mexico when he was six and was undocumented until 1998. Alonso, an Army veteran who served in Baghdad and Fallujah, told the committee that allowing students to attend Virginia colleges would show that the state "recognized and maximized their potential."

THE DEVELOPMENT, RELIEF, AND EDUCATION
FOR ALIEN MINORS ACT (DREAM ACT), UTAH

Among the new settlement sites researched for this handbook, only the State of Utah took a landmark step by allowing undocumented immigrant students to pay in-state tuition while attending public universities and colleges. The Development, Relief, and Education for Alien Minors (DREAM) Act legislation was approved under the provision that undocumented students must be enrolled in a public high school for at least three years before attending college. The bill advanced in part through the efforts of Silvia Salguero, an undocumented high school student in Park City who dropped out of the University of Utah to work as a housekeeper. Salguero was in no position to pay $8,800 in tuition while the resident students were paying $2,900. Working with teachers, legislators, members of Congress, and presidents of Utah's universities, Salguero and other immigrant students established a precedent in the nation.

Since 2001, eight other states—Texas, California, Washington, New York, Oklahoma, Illinois, Kansas, and New Mexico—have passed laws permitting certain undocumented students who have attended and graduated from their primary and secondary schools to pay the same tuition as their classmates at public institutions of higher education. A majority of America's undocumented immigrants live in these states.

Senator Orrin Hatch has proposed Utah's version as a model for national legislation. To qualify for immigration relief under the Senate's DREAM Act, a student must have been brought to the U.S. more than five years ago when s/he was 15 years old or younger and must be able to demonstrate good moral character. Under the DREAM Act, once such a student graduates from high school, s/he would be permitted to apply for conditional status, which would authorize up to six years of legal residence. During the six-year period, the student would be required to graduate from a two-year college, complete at least two years toward a four-year degree, or serve in the U.S. military for at least two years. Permanent residence would be granted at the end of the six-year period if these requirements have been met and if the student has continued to maintain good moral character. The DREAM Act also eliminates a federal provision that discourages states from providing in-state tuition to their undocumented immigrant student residents, thus restoring full authority to the states to determine state college and university fees.

Support for the DREAM Act has been steadily growing since it was first introduced in 2001 during the 107th Congress. In May 2006, for the first time, the DREAM Act passed the full Senate as part of the Comprehensive Immigration Reform Act of 2006 (S. 2611). There was a high probability that it would have passed the House if brought up for a vote in 2006, but the House leadership neglected to bring it to a vote. The notion of facilitating education to this population continues to attract bipartisan support and as of February 2007 enjoyed the strong backing of the House and Senate leadership and all of the relevant committee chairs.[5]

NOTES

1. Randy Capps, Michael Fix, Julie Murray, Jason Ost, Jeffrey S. Passel, Shinta Herwantoro, *The New Demography of American Schools: Immigration and the No Child Left Behind Act* (Washington, DC: Urban Institute, 2005).

2. Raleigh Bailey "New Immigrant Communities in the North Carolina Piedmont Triad: Integration Issues and Challenges," in *Beyond the Gateway: Immigrants in a Changing America*, ed. Elżbieta Goździak, and Susan F. Martin (Lanham, MD: Lexington Books, 2005), 57–86.

3. Art Hansen, "Black and White and the Other: International Immigration and Change in Metropolitan Atlanta," in *Beyond the Gateway: Immigrants in a Changing America*, ed. Elżbieta Goździak, and Susan F. Martin (Lanham, MD: Lexington Books, 2005), 87–109.

4. Brigit Schulte, "Trapped between Two Languages," *Washington Post*, June 9, 2002.

5. National Immigration Law Center, *"Dream Act: Basic Information,"* February 2007. Available at http://www.nilc.org/immlawpolicy/DREAM/dream_basic_info_0406.pdf.

6

Facilitating Immigrant Access to Culturally Sensitive and Linguistically Appropriate Health Care

Access to regular and comprehensive health care is essential to effective integration of immigrants. Investment in culturally sensitive and linguistically appropriate health services for newcomers early in the settlement process increases immigrants' ability to integrate and minimizes costly public interventions at later stages. Health programs that increase accessibility and continuity of care constitute good public policy because they save public money and strengthen a valuable human resource. Yet, under current law, immigrants who arrived in the United States after August 1996 are barred for five years from receiving health benefits under Medicaid or State Children's Health Insurance Program (SCHIP). Even taxpaying families with pregnant women and children are affected. These restrictions, enacted as part of the Personal Responsibility and Work Opportunities Reconciliation Act of 1996 (PREWORA), have left a large hole in the social safety net for new Americans. Since permanent residents and other legal immigrants lost their eligibility for many benefits, Medicaid for low-income non-citizens decreased from 19 percent in 1995 to 15 percent in 1999.[1]

Two key factors affecting immigrants' access to health care are lack of insurance and insufficient capacity of safety net providers. According to Census Bureau data, the foreign born are more than twice as likely as U.S.-born individuals to lack health insurance. The Census Bureau's Current Population Survey (CPS) data for March 2002 indicate that, nationally, 33 percent of foreign-born residents have neither private nor public health insurance coverage, compared to 13 percent of U.S.-born residents. Of those living in poverty, 26 percent of U.S.-born residents do not have health insurance, compared to 55 percent of the foreign born.

The 2000 Medical Expenditure Panel Survey indicates that high rates of unstable medical coverage are especially likely to affect Hispanic children in low-income families. Forty-four percent of Hispanic children were uninsured in 2000, compared with one-third of U.S. children in low-income families. According to a Children's Defense Fund analysis, the percentage of immigrant (non-citizen) children without health insurance increased from 39.3 percent in 2000, to 41.6 percent in 2001, and 42.1 percent in 2002. By contrast, the percentage of all children who are uninsured did not change between 2001 and 2002, remaining at 11.6 percent.[2]

Immigrant women of childbearing age are also at risk for insufficient health care coverage. More than 50 percent of foreign-born women are of childbearing age.[3] Although publicly funded health care programs such as Medicaid cover the cost of delivery, most uninsured immigrant women have no access to prenatal care.

Sixty-one percent of Hispanics aged fifty to sixty-four were uninsured in 2000, compared with 41 percent of their peers in the general population. One-quarter of Hispanics age fifty to sixty-four went without necessary care in the same year, either skipping medical tests or failing to fill prescriptions. The uninsured tend to neglect preventive care, use the emergency room for primary care, and delay seeking treatment until problems become acute and care is much more costly. Our research in Winchester, Virginia, highlights the grim consequences of the lack of proper medical care. Winchester saw three infants and one mother from the Latino immigrant community lose their lives during childbirth in 2001 and 2002 because the families could not afford proper pre-natal care.

Language and cultural differences also impede immigrants' access to health care services. Many non-English speaking immigrants, including those with insurance, struggle to negotiate the complex terrain of the American health care system. Many studies have shown that lack of language skills is a significant barrier to receiving adequate care. In one survey, Latino children had much less access to medical care than Caucasian children, but the gap was negligible once their parents' English language proficiency was comparable to that of white parents.[4] Too often immigrants with limited English language proficiency are forced to rely on untrained interpreters. Miscommunication and poor translation of medical terms can lead to an onset of otherwise preventable diseases or even death. Young family members are frequently called on to serve as interpreters, which can lead to violation of privacy and embarrassment.

Federal and state laws crafted to remedy this situation have not always produced the intended results. Title VI of the Civil Rights Act of 1964, which prohibits discrimination based on national origin, has been interpreted to mean that federally funded services (including health care) must ensure that individuals with limited English language proficiency have access to linguistically appropriate services. Unfortunately, the provisions are not always enforced, impeding immigrants' utilization of available health care services. Language barriers lead newcomers to postpone seeking care and limit comprehension of diagnoses and required treatments, thereby reducing compliance with prescribed medications and treatment regiments. Language barriers have also been associated with increased hospital admissions and lower patient satisfaction.

Research indicates that language barriers also have a number of indirect effects on immigrant patients and the health care system itself. Ethnic minorities who are not proficient in English are underrepresented in both clinical and health service research. This exclusion means that study results cannot be generalized to the entire population and that less is known about specific risk factors, the prevalence of certain diseases, and the response to treatment among newcomer groups. Language barriers also affect provider effectiveness and satisfaction. Some evidence indicates that language barriers may increase health care costs through their impact on services and health outcomes.

Immigrants' use of health care services is also affected by cultural issues such as lack of sensitivity on the part of health care providers and newcomers' attitudes about disease and illness. Unfamiliarity among many health care providers with the backgrounds and experiences of their patients makes it difficult for them to diagnose and develop appropriate treatment plans. In many immigrant communities there is a great stigma attached to certain diseases, particularly mental illness, which makes it difficult to seek help from American health care providers. Conversely, many American mental health care providers have a tendency to medicalize the suffering of refugees and immigrants and are unwilling to consider indigenous healing strategies.

Paradoxically, recent immigrants are often healthier than their counterparts that have been in the United States longer. However, as newcomers begin to integrate and adopt the American way of life, their health status begins to converge with that of the general U.S. population.[5] Immigrants' health behaviors—including eating habits, food choices, and physical activity patterns—change, often leading to negative health outcomes: increased risk for a number of disease and metabolic abnormalities such as coronary heart disease, hyperinsulinemia, insulin resistance, type 2 diabetes, certain cancers, and osteoarthritis.

Policymakers, service providers, and community leaders interviewed in the course of this study were quite aware of what often seemed like insurmountable obstacles to immigrants' health care access and utilization. Nevertheless, many communities succeeded in designing and implementing very creative strategies. Some created international clinics catering to multicultural and multilingual patient population or established specialized health care programs for low-income, uninsured immigrants; others focused on advocacy, health literacy and health promotion. Still others focused on training refugee and immigrant health care workers. Many communities established quality-training programs for bilingual and bi-cultural medical interpreters.

INTERNATIONAL CLINICS

Localities with a large number of newcomers and an established history of providing health care services to refugees and immigrants have been well positioned to establish comprehensive international clinics at local hospitals. Economy of scale was a critical element of this strategy. Localities with smaller immigrant populations were less likely to adopt this approach. However, health care practitioners in cities with larger concentration of the foreign born encouraged providers in settlements with more recent and smaller waves of immigrants to consider this strategy down the road.

HealthPartners Regions Center for International Health, St. Paul, Minnesota

The HealthPartners Regions Center for International Health, located on the Regions Hospital Campus in St. Paul, Minnesota, is an excellent example of a health care facility for ambulatory patients who come from all corners of the world. The Center has been an innovator in delivering cross-cultural health care since its inception in 1980. In most ambulatory facilities, non-English speaking patients are treated alongside the general population. Clinicians and other providers do their best to communicate, but for some it can be a frustrating process that slows down the patient flow. Regions Hospital has taken the unusual step of creating an international clinic specifically for newcomer patients.

The guiding philosophy of the Center is to meet its patients on their own terms. In order to accomplish this goal, the clinic provides holistic, culturally competent care that meets the physical, mental, and social service needs of its patients. A multidisciplinary focus brings together a team of internists, psychologists, psychiatrists, physician assistants, nurse practitioners, nurse midwives, nurses, medical assistants, and social workers into one clinic.

To serve many distinct refugee and immigrant groups efficiently and effectively, professionally trained medical interpreters are on-site to assist Vietnamese, Cambodian, Hmong, Lao, French, Spanish, Oromo, and Somali patients. At the time of our research, there were 12 full-time and 22 part-time trained interpreters. All were graduates of Bridging the Gap Medical Interpretation Program (*see below*). The availability of a pool of well-trained interpreters allows for medication labels can be printed in multiple languages, and medication boxes to be dispensed to reduce medication errors due to language barriers. Health education brochures and videotapes in several languages are also available at no charge.

According to the Center's social worker, access to health care may not be the primary concern for newly arrived refugees or immigrants. Often they need help addressing language and employment issues. A full-time social worker is on staff at the Center to provide assistance in managing integration concerns. She and other staff members actively reach out to the Southeast Asian, African, Russian, and Latino communities, presenting health literacy and cross-cultural health education where community members live and gather.

At the time of our site visit, the Center was enjoying a three-year grant from the Medtronic Foundation, its largest award ever for health care programs assisting refugees and immigrants. The grant helped fund community outreach as well as two Somali interpreters and a social worker/case manager. David Etzwiler, director of community affairs at the Medtronic Foundation, noted that "When competent and caring people commit themselves to improving the lives of others, amazing things happen; as a funder, you really want to be a part of that. The center delivers on every grant dollar it receives."[6]

Bilingual and bicultural staff member are key to the Center's cross-cultural competence. The Center actively mentors, recruits, and hires bilingual and bicultural workers at all levels of expertise. Their training and life experiences foster respect for each patient's needs and preferences, including use of alternative health care and non-traditional healers.

Patricia Walker, MD, is medical director at the Center. Born in Thailand and raised in Southeast Asia, she speaks Thai, Lao, and Khmer as well as Spanish. She became interested in international medicine when she attended Mayo Medical School. Dr. Walker offered insights on how health care providers can start their own international clinics or refine their care of immigrant patients. To prepare to serve New Americans, Dr. Walker said, ambulatory facilities must hire medically trained professional interpreters; pay attention to the layout and décor as well as equipment (including multilingual telephone lines) of the clinic to make it accessible and culturally sensitive; hire bilingual and bicultural staff from the front desk all the way to the doctors; share expertise as a way of expanding horizons among health care providers; take a multidisciplinary approach to ambulatory health care, including internists, psychologists, psychiatrists, pediatricians, nurse practitioners, and nurse midwives; promote cultural competency; and recognize that community involvement is a cornerstone of international care.

The Center's walls are decorated with pictures of patients who became U.S. citizens as well as posters that reflect the cultural diversity of immigrants seeking care in the clinic. The receptionist who greeted us was multilingual, but apologized that she did not speak Polish. The interpreters have their own answering system with greetings and messages pre-recorded in the particular language they speak. If need be, patients can be put on a three-way telephone call with their physician.

In addition to interpreters, the Center also employs bilingual and bicultural medical personnel, including a Cambodian as well as a Russian psychologist, a Vietnamese psychiatrist, and an Indian pediatrician. Some of the professional staff are refugees themselves and serve as excellent role models. Dr. Walker noted that hiring bilingual and bicultural staff required attention to advertising.

> Make sure that you advertise at minority health fairs and ethnic TV and radio media. If your human resources staff helps you advertise, you have to be able to tell them where to place the ads.
>
> —Patricia F. Walker, MD

Dr. Walker insists on a multidisciplinary approach to ambulatory health care for New Americans and says that an international clinic must incorporate social work and mental health services. She proposes to look at foreign-born patients not as problems, but as patients that need a provider who is also going to be their advocate. Dr. Walker stresses that ethnic community involvement is a cornerstone of immigrant health care. The face of America is changing. "Stay humble and know you're always learning," she said.

SPECIALIZED HEALTH SERVICES

Other programs followed a strategy of developing specialized health care services for different groups of low-income immigrants. The best example of this approach is Partners in Perinatal Care, a program developed in Winchester, Virginia, for uninsured women.

Partners in Perinatal Care, Winchester, Virginia

Between 1990 and 2000 Winchester, an independent city of 25,000 residents, located in Frederick County, experienced the highest proportionate growth in Hispanic population in the Washington, DC, metropolitan area. According to the 2000 Census, Winchester's Hispanic population grew by nearly 600 percent between 1990 and 2000. The increase from 219 individuals in 1990 to 1,527 in 2000 indicates that Hispanics represented approximately 6.5 percent of the city's population.[7]

As more newcomers have settled permanently in the area, the health care system has come under increasing pressure to provide health services to the Latino community. The number one health care need among the local Latino population was prenatal care; more than 60 percent of the surveyed Latinos were under 35 years of age and included a high percentage of women of childbearing age. Before 2002, all expectant women in Winchester were eligible for one visit to an obstetrician in the Health Department. Under state guidelines, the Health Department was obligated to refer them to a private OBGYN provider. While there were three different obstetricians in Winchester, they all required approximately $500 as a deposit from anyone lacking private health insurance or Medicaid eligibility. A follow-up visit cost another $500 and every subsequent visit came with a price tag of about $180. At the time of our research, it cost anywhere from $2,700 to $3,000 to have a baby in Winchester.

Many of the expectant immigrant mothers, who were often young and unemployed, did not have the money to pay for prenatal care. Those who worked, usually in low-wage, entry-level positions, or were supported by husbands, boyfriends or other family members, did not have sufficient income to cover a $3,000 birth expense. As a result, pregnant women were arriving at the emergency room in labor with no prenatal care, or at most, the single visit to the Health Department. This has had drastic consequences: three infants and one mother from the Latino immigrant community lost their lives during childbirth in 2001 and 2002.

The deaths revealed the weakness of the existing health care system and prompted concerned immigrant advocates, members of Latino Connection, to approach Valley Health System to establish a prenatal care program that would ensure access and improve the health of immigrant mothers and infants in the area. Through a community-based effort initiated by a bilingual nurse from the Winchester Health Department, Valley Health System obtained a $570,860 grant from the Department of Health Resources and Services Administration (HRSA) and the Partners in Perinatal Care (PIPC) program was born in November 2002. A full-time bilingual nurse and part-time administrator were hired along with a transport aide, and three bilingual *doulas*, or birthing assistants.

The program serves pregnant, uninsured women who are ineligible for Medicaid and unable to afford proper care out of pocket. The program provides transportation to the health care facilities and interpretation during prenatal visits, delivery, and postpartum as well as newborn care. It also provides assistance with Medicaid and birth certificate applications. The goal is to provide a continuum of quality prenatal care as well as an opportunity for information sharing between health care providers, community advocates, and client groups.

As of August 2005, PIPC transitioned from a grant-funded to community-funded organization. Patients are referred through the Valley Health System. Katy Pitcock, the program director, estimates that about 300 women have participated in the program in 2004 and 2005; of course, the benefits extend to a much larger number of family and community members.

Healthy Families of Northern Shenandoah Valley, Winchester, Virginia

A private, community-based collaborative with about twenty sites in Virginia, Healthy Families works with young families on a voluntary basis to support positive parenting through information, referral and home-visiting services. Family support workers are available to work with qualified new parents before the child is born and stay with the family until the child is ready to enter school. At the time of our research, the Winchester site had ten staff members, but only one Spanish-speaking bilingual and bicultural worker. Given the time demands of working with foreign-born monolingual mothers, the Spanish-speaking worker had her caseload reduced considerably and was working with eight Mexican single mothers. Since then, another Spanish-speaking bicultural worker joined the staff and the program is currently serving 75 families, including 15 immigrant families. Services include transportation to medical appointments, immunization tracking, and developmental education, and testing.

A bilingual staff member interviewed for this study indicated that many of the first-time Latino mothers benefit greatly from home visits and consultations provided by the program as they often lack the support system of their own mothers and grandmothers who stayed behind in Mexico. Most of them are single mothers. Many of the fathers are also not involved in raising the newborn babies, either because it is culturally inappropriate or because the young mothers are not married to the fathers of their children.

ALTERNATIVES MODES OF SERVICE DELIVERY

Across the new settlement sites some service providers and community leaders have developed creative ways of delivering health care services. The People's Clinic in Park City, Utah, uses a medical van staffed with volunteer physicians, nurses, and medical interpreters to provide both primary and specialized care, while the Cambodian community in Greensboro, North Carolina, offers mental health and psychosocial services out of a Buddhist temple serving Cambodian refugees.

People's Health Clinic, Park City, Utah

The People's Health Clinic (PHC) is a community-based 501(c) 3 non-profit organization. It is the only medical facility of its kind in Utah and one of very few in the United States. PHC was created to provide health care for residents of Summit and Wasatch Counties after a one-time health fair drew more than 750 people, highlighting the need for affordable health care. The event was a catalyst for the opening in April 2000 of a mobile clinic or a 35-foot van that traveled Summit and Wasatch counties for almost four years delivering primary care to uninsured families who live and work in the areas. Following its inception, the clinic logged more than 3,500 patient visits in its first three years. In 2002, 91 percent of the patients were Hispanic; 65 percent were women and 20 percent were children, and 89 percent lived in Park City. Nearly all were working poor with multiple jobs that did not provide basic health insurance. The largest "treatment group" were women receiving prenatal care.

"At first blush, a free clinic might seem superfluous in a place where it would be easy to conclude people are more worried about the next Brie shipment than where their inoculations are coming from," wrote a local newspaper.[8] As Park City has expanded its status as one of the world's premier destination resort towns, it has attracted a growing number of largely Hispanic service workers. The back-of-the-line workers, the cooks, dishwashers, and housekeepers working in the resort struggle to make ends meet in a playground for the rich and famous. In the early 2000, Hispanics comprised roughly 20 percent of the Park City population.

The van that was the original mobile clinic costs about $250,000, but it was a demo and was purchased for $175,000; the funds came entirely through private donations. In fact, creative fund-raising has been the hallmark of the clinic. At some point PHC auctioned four skis and lodging packages on eBay, one package at a time. All three local resorts donated lift tickets and Deer Valley, R&R Properties, and Snow Flower Condominiums donated lodgings. The only cost PHC incurred was the cost of listing the offered goods on the auction website. Posting the vacation packages on eBay required less effort than organizing dinners and silent auctions in town. However, both begin with soliciting donations from private businesses. Using eBay also involved a learning curve, but had fewer details to attend to. Fundraising on the Internet is not without drawbacks. PHC has learned through trial and error how to manipulate the new fund-raising medium to gain the most profit. Timing, for example, was crucial. When the first vacation package was put on eBay in November nobody was bidding on it. However, in December, people had skiing on their minds and things moved much faster.

eBay is not the only fund-raising mode used by PHC. The Jump In! Youth Leadership Group from a local high school planned, organized and promoted a walkathon and a silent auction which brought in $4,500 profit. After volunteering at PHC, a local pediatrics nurse practitioner and her husband held a *Charity Stomp*. The event included dinner, dancing, and an auction and raised $6,700. The Phat Bottom Girls, a group of five young women from Park City, completed a grueling 24-hour mountain endurance race and raised $1,500. A Park City resident and a Delta Airlines pilot took an initiative to write letters to his fellow pilots residing in the area asking for a direct contribution to PHC's operating costs. Several area pilots responded with generous donations. In April 2003, PHC launched the "Partners in Caring" program designed to involve local businesses by offering various options to contribute to the clinic, through the form of a health care partner for a day, a week, a month. The program was launched at the spring meeting of the Park City Area Lodging Association and was received enthusiastically.

> Volunteering at PHC is a great clinical experience in preparation to attend a Physician Assistant program. I truly believe in the cause of assisting prenatal women who do not have other means. It also allows me to understand the demographics of Park City and contribute to the community in which I live.
>
> —Alison Waterbury, Emergency Medical
> Technician and Medical Assistant
>
> I got into PHC through a friend as a desire to use my Spanish. I get to meet many different people, learn about the patients, and feel like I am making a small difference in some people's lives.
>
> —Mike Thomas, pre-med student, BYU
>
> Volunteering is a way of life for me. It is a part of my family, and I care about this organization very much. Without the PHC, most of the patients would not receive any care.
>
> —Donna Fisher, Physician

PHC lists every donor in their newsletters and is very savvy about using local media to cover the contributions of donors and volunteers. According to one newsletter, volunteers are the clinic's most important resource. The PHC volunteer corps includes physicians, physician assistants, nurse practitioners, interpreters, phlebotomists, and specialists who welcome patient referrals from the clinic.

La semana de los no asegurados, a week of the uninsured, was celebrated in March 2003. The celebration was part of the national campaign launched by former presidents Gerald Ford and Jimmy Carter, to focus attention on the plight of uninsured Americans. Donna McCaller, Executive Director of PHC, wrote a guest editorial for *The Park Record* on the issue of uninsured, low-income residents of Park City and surrounding counties.

In 2004 the mobile clinic van was sold and PHC moved to new stationary quarters. Patients have a full waiting room with a receptionist's desk.

The intake area is tucked away from the main traffic path, giving patients more privacy. The crown jewel of the new space is a trio of examination rooms. The Intermountain Health Care donated the cabinets, examination tables and other pieces from its surplus supplies. The space also includes a room for office work.

The PHC is currently the only source of non-emergency health care for many uninsured individuals and families in the area. The clinic offers general and family care on Monday nights and prenatal and women's care on Wednesday nights. Patients receive a variety of medical services and health care for needs ranging from allergies and rashes to seizures and advanced diabetes. The clinic provides medical consultations, prescription medications, free vitamins and translators to those in need of medical help. The PHC also pays for laboratory work, x-rays, ultrasound tests, and referrals, when required.

The Greensboro Buddhist Center, Greensboro, North Carolina

In 1985, the Khmer Aid Group of the North Carolina Triad established a Buddhist temple in Greensboro to provide culturally appropriate healing services to the many suffering Cambodian refugees resettled in the area. The temple, assisted by Lutheran Family Services and supported by a grant from the Z. Smith Reynolds Foundation, has become an invaluable resource for community organizing and heritage preservation. It has also anchored a support network for more than five hundred Buddhist refugee and immigrant families in the Carolinas and Virginia. The rural setting of the Greensboro Buddhist Center enhances its serene atmosphere despite its location in one of North Carolina's largest metropolises.

The Center heals the wounds of the war and the lingering effects of the genocide committed by Pol Pot and the Khmer Rouge by offering a supportive spiritual environment to Cambodian refugees and their families. Each week the Center holds a Buddhist service beginning at nine o'clock. Up to two hundred regular members attend and stay for lunch, dharma lessons, and recreation. In addition, the temple holds larger monthly services in Thai, Lao, or Cambodian traditions that attract four or five hundred devotees. Although the monks (including the temple's Thai-born spiritual leader, Phramaha Somsak Sambimb) speak English, the services are held in Lao or Khmer. Led by the three resident monks, the services include chanting of the sutras and offerings of food to the monks. Interpreters are available for these who don't understand Lao or Khmer. The temple also sponsors two dance groups as well as a summer camp for children and provides opportunities for socializing at its nearby lake, volleyball court, and gardens.

On the day of our site visit, Somsak was lecturing at one of the local schools, the dance group was holding a rehearsal, several monks were gardening in an organic garden on the outskirts of the temple complex, and a group of Cambodian women were selling homemade lunch and carrying on an animated conversation in Khmer.

FACILITATING ACCESS TO HEALTH CARE SERVICES

There were several examples of programs facilitating or enhancing access to health care services. The strategies included utilization of health promoters recruited from among target refugee and immigrant populations, and provision of interpretation and translation services to the foreign born seeking medical assistance. In many instances the health advocates played both roles skillfully.

Immigrant Health ACCESS Project, Greensboro, North Carolina

Hospitals eager to reduce emergency room care for immigrants and refugees have sought ways to treat non-emergency health needs outside the hospital system. A local foundation, the Moses Cone-Wesley Long Community Health Foundation, supported the Center for New North Carolinians (CNCC) at the University of North Carolina at Greensboro (UNCG) to provide Lay Health Advisors (LHAs) to various refugee and immigrant communities in the area. Building on the immigrant network created in Guilford County by the AmeriCorps ACCESS Project, the Immigrant Health ACCESS Project hired and trained bilingual and bicultural health advisors from targeted communities. The advisors were charged with facilitating immigrants' integration into the local health care system by providing interpretation and transportation as necessary, conducting health education activities, and advising providers on immigrant health and cultural traditions. The advisors initially included Latino, Somali, Sudanese, Montagnard, and Laotian representatives, but are now expanding to include representatives of other newcomer groups.

Promotoras de Salud, Winchester, Virginia

As a community, Winchester has been challenged for years to dispel fears regarding the American health care system and foster immigrant trust. A program directed by a Salvadoran member of the Latino Connection has begun to address this issue. Through a federal grant and a four-way partnership among Valley Health System, James Madison University, Shenandoah University, and the Lord Fairfax Health District, members of the local Winchester/Frederick County Hispanic community have been trained as *promotoras de salud* (health educators). This program, which began in 1999 in Harrisonburg, is viewed by the community as a positive step in educating the newcomer community on pertinent health-related issues and making the sometimes daunting local health care system more accessible. Since the program's inception in 1999, it has provided 750 referrals, responded to 377 interpretation/translation requests, and recorded 7,887 health education encounters.

Approximately 30 Hispanic women are trained each year. The program involves 40 hours of instruction over a 10-week period and provides culturally sensitive training in health promotion, diseases, and injury prevention. Topics covered in the course—offered twice a year—include diabetes, HIV/AIDS, tuberculosis, cancer, and heart disease, as well as overall health care information, such as where to receive treatment. Participants are also advised as to which doctors speak Spanish, and who will provide interpreters. In addition to performing basic health services, graduates can also explain to non-English speaking residents where to go for help, assist them in enrolling for Medicaid or other insurance programs, and distribute health materials in Spanish. Classes are taught by local nurses and educators.[9]

Partners in the project include the poultry industry (Cargill, Tyson Foods, Pilgrim's Pride Corporation), Harrisonburg Area Hispanic Services Council, James Madison and Eastern Mennonite University Nursing Departments, Harrisonburg-Rockingham Health Department, Catholic Church of the Blessed Sacrament, Asbury United Methodist Church, Rockingham Memorial Hospital and the United Way of Harrisonburg.

Multicultural Community Health Promoters Program, Clarkson, GA

Health disparities experienced by immigrants and refugees are most striking among women. In response to requests from refugee women, the DeKalb County Board of Health trained fifteen community health promoters (CHPs) representing five refugee communities in Clarkston, Georgia, where one-third of the population is foreign born. The project is a collaborative effort of three partner agencies, the Refugee Women's Network (RWN), Clarkston Community Center, and the DeKalb County Board of Health. All three partners worked together to write the grant that secured the funding for this effort. RWN took responsibility for recruitment and communication with the women. The DCBOH was responsible for the training and implementation of the program. The CCC provided the venue, stipend payments, and administrative oversight. The Center for Diseases Control (CDC) provided a Preventive Medicine Resident who spent her residency assisting in the training design as well as developing and overseeing project evaluation.

The initial financial support came in the form of a $150,000 grant over a two-year period from the Healthcare Georgia Foundation. The funds

supported a part-time project director, development of the training program and training manual, as well as a small stipend for each promoter.
The CHPs committed to reaching 40 families during each year. The program trains refugee and immigrant health promoters to conduct health
education classes in their native language; serve as a health information
resource and liaison; advocate for better health care for their community;
and empower community members to advocate for their health rights.
Apparently, the project made a very good impression on the federal Office
of Refugee Resettlement (ORR) which expressed an interest in supporting
the efforts in the near future.

MEDICAL INTERPRETATION TRAINING

> We've learned the critical importance of medically trained professional inter-
> preters. The use of family members, children, neighbors, and community
> leaders is not only fraught with significant medical and legal concerns, but
> also quality-of-care concerns.
>
> If you are seeing new Americans, you should have professionally trained in-
> terpreters. If the amount of patients you have doesn't warrant hiring your own
> staff, you can contract out for that service. Contract with agencies that provide
> interpreters. In a big city, these are often run by entrepreneurs. The second
> choice is to use AT&T or MCI interpreters.
>
> —Patricia F. Walker, MD

Even in cases where monetary costs are not prohibitive, language barriers
have obstructed access to adequate health care. Traditionally, many health
care facilities have relied on a limited number of bilingual personnel, family members, or a list of paid but untrained interpreters to assist their non-
English speaking patients. As newcomer populations have grown, however,
health care providers have sought permanent solutions to medical interpretation challenges.

Bridging the Gap Medical Interpreter Training Program, Seattle

Two of the groups interviewed in this study, Valley Health System in the
Shenandoah Valley and the Center for International Health at Regions Hospital in St. Paul, Minnesota, use the Bridging the Gap Medical Interpreter Training Program. Offered through the Seattle-based non-profit Cross-Cultural
Health Care Program, the forty-hour course trains interpreters on issues including communication styles, medical terminology, professionalism, ethics,

confidentiality, health care, and insurance. To qualify for the course bilingual speakers must pass oral and written comprehension tests in two languages and possess basic knowledge of medical terms and common diseases.

"Effective Use of Interpreters," Winchester, Virginia

As much as trained interpreters improve communication, medical professionals need to know how to use them effectively. The Latino Connection in Winchester, Virginia, addressed this need by developing a companion program, "Effective Use of Interpreters," which teaches English only speakers to make the best use of interpreters and judge the quality of interpreted communication. This training has been provided to local schools and several hospital departments and was scheduled for social services and other community agencies.

TRAINING BILINGUAL AND BICULTURAL HEALTH CARE PROVIDERS

A well-trained bilingual and bicultural staff is essential to facilitating newcomers' access to culturally sensitive and linguistically appropriate health care services. Several localities, including Minnesota and Georgia, have developed creative medical training and recertification programs to accomplish this goal.

Medical Careers for New Americans Program, St. Paul, Minnesota

The Medical Careers for New Americans Program at the International Institute of Minnesota offers vocational training for immigrants interested in employment in the health care field. The three components of the program—Nursing Assistant Training, Medical Careers Advancement, and Academic Skills Training—help immigrants climb the career ladder in the health care industry from entry-level to advanced positions through educational counseling, financial assistance, certification courses, career analysis, and job search skills training.

Nursing Assistant Training Program

The program follows state-approved curriculum for training nursing assistants and provides vocational English language instruction. Its lengthy duration (six, eight and eleven-weeks) gives students time to master other skills, including conflict resolution and resume preparation. Students are certified to work in nursing homes and other health care facilities in Minnesota.

Classes meet Monday through Friday from 8:30 a.m. to 2:30 p.m. An employment specialist helps certified students find jobs.

To be eligible for this program, applicants must be refugees or asylees, permanent residents, or naturalized U.S. citizens; speak and understand English at a functional level; receive public assistance or work at a low-income job or be unemployed; provide their own transportation, daycare, and uniform; be in good physical condition; and be willing to enter the labor force immediately after training.

From its inception in 1990 through 2002, the program enrolled 739 students. Of those, 674 have completed the program and 657 have been certified as nursing assistants and were employed by sixty different health care facilities in the Twin City Metropolitan Area.

Medical Careers Advancement Program

The Medical Careers Advancement Program helps immigrants progress within the health care field from entry-level to advanced positions. Program participants receive guidance in selection of the appropriate medical career and educational institution, counseling, financial assistance (to allow them to work part-time while pursuing the training), and development of skills such as career analysis, organizational skills, job search skills, and workplace skills. Participants are also eligible for support through the on-site Academic Skills Training Program (*see below*). The Medical Careers Advancement Program is funded by the Greater Twin Cities United Way, the McKnight Foundation, the St. Paul Foundation, the F.R. Bigelow Foundation, the Otto Bremer Foundation, and the Department of Employment & Economic Security.

Academic Skills

To help ensure the success of students enrolled in the medical careers program, the Academic Skills Training program offers academic support to participants. First, Academic ESL classes are available to students who are refugees, asylees, permanent residents or naturalized citizens. Second, a series of one to two-week Academic Skills Workshops are offered to address common skill gaps. Workshops include Strategies for Academic Success, College Writing and Research Skills, The Language of Medicine, and Effective Pronunciation of American English. Finally, tutoring in planning or editing college papers and in basic math is available by appointment to participants in the Medical Career Advancement Program who are enrolled in college. This program is funded by the McKnight Foundation and the Jay and Rose Phillips Foundation.

Refugee Healthcare and Medical Mentorship Project, Atlanta

Founded in 1981, Lutheran Services of Georgia (LSGA, formerly Lutheran Ministries of Georgia) is a social service agency, which combines the resources of staff, financial donors, governmental agencies, volunteers, and Lutheran congregations in an effort to bring programs and services to the people of Georgia. LSGA administers more than twenty programs in the areas of adoption, foster care, family services, refugee resettlement, disaster response, youth employment, and support for disabled adults.

LSGA launched the Refugee Healthcare and Medical Mentorship Project (RHEMP) to assist refugee and immigrant professionals with training and previous work experience in the health care field to re-enter their profession upon arrival in the United States. The goal of the program is to prepare professionals for health care jobs through onsite work experience, professional development training workshops, re-certification assistance, and vocational training. A decision by the nearby DeKalb Medical Center, a project partner, to build a $67 million hospital was an impetus to launch the project. The medical center foresees a need for a multicultural, multilingual staff to attend to the increasingly diverse community in the Atlanta area. At the time of our research, twenty-six clients were enrolled in the program.

NOTES

1. Grantmakers in Health Resource Center. 2000. "Different World: Immigrant Access to Culturally Appropriate Health Care." Available online at www.gih.org.
2. U.S. Census Bureau press release, September 30, 2003.
3. Dianne Schmidley, "The Foreign-Born Population in the United States: March 2002," *Current Population Reports* (Washington, DC: U.S. Census Bureau, 2003), 20–539.
4. Robin M. Weinick and Nancy A. Krauss, "Racial and Ethnic Differences in Children's Access to Care," *American Journal of Public Health* 90 (November 2000): 1771–1774.
5. Grantmakers in Health. "For the Benefit of All: Ensuring Immigrant Health and Well-Being." Issue Brief No. 24, November 2005.
6. Regions Hospital Foundation. "Passion to Heal: 2001 Annual Report."
7. U.S. Census Bureau, 1990 Census and 2000 Census.
8. Gib Twyman, "Health Van's a Paradox in Paradise," *Deseret News.*
9. Dan Telvock, "Graduates Bridge Gap to Save Lives," *Winchester Star,* November 25, 2002.

7

Creating Homeownership Opportunities for Immigrants[1]

Homeownership is perceived as a major milestone in immigrant integration, in feeling part of the community, in becoming American. The longer immigrants live in the United States, the more likely they are to purchase homes. The number of homes owned by foreign-born owners is projected to grow by 2.2 million between 1995 and 2010.

Homeownership rates for immigrants are closely related to immigration status, income, and length of residence in the United States. Seventy three percent of naturalized citizens who entered the U.S. before 1979 are homeowners; their rate of homeownership significantly exceeds the native homeownership rate of 68 percent. The rate is dramatically lower for those immigrants who have not been naturalized and for all immigrants who arrived in the United States since 1984.

Hispanics have become the nation's largest minority group. Today 50 percent of surveyed Hispanics are foreign born, up from 36 percent in 1990. While homeownership rates among foreign born Hispanics climbed from 37 percent in 1994 to more than 40 percent in 1999 and 49.5 percent in 2005, homeownership rates for foreign born lag well behind (approximately 15 percent) those of the native born (see Table 1.7). Why is this part of the American dream out of reach for so many immigrants?

Several major barriers contribute to immigrants' relatively low homeownership rates:

- Many immigrants bring with them old-country knowledge and customs regarding home-buying and financial institutions. Often they distrust banks and financial institutions and do not open checking or savings accounts. Many immigrants do not have an understanding of the credit approval process and requirements. Those who come from societies where a large down payment is the rule assume the same applies in the United States.

- Limited ability to understand, speak and read English keeps immigrants outside the mainstream home-buying industry. To overcome this limitation, immigrants sometimes turn to "cultural brokers"— some legitimate, but others not.
- At the point when they might like to purchase a home, many immigrants cannot demonstrate conventional credit histories or document earnings. By custom, they often prefer not to use credit cards. Although they pay rent, their names might not be on their leases.
- Many financial institutions use conventional tools to measure credit worthiness. Immigrants often are deemed ineligible for financing when their conventionally measured assets and income are screened by computer. In many cases, immigrants' cash payments for their work off the books do not register under conventional approaches.
- Conventional mortgage products often are out of financial reach for low-income immigrants, even during periods of relatively low mortgage rates.
- Affordable housing, particularly in high-cost urban markets, is difficult to find.

Innovative organizations and progressive leaders in the homeownership industry have developed effective strategies to overcome these barriers and reach this unique first-time home-buyer market, including:

- Recruitment programs to increase the number of bilingual staff;
- Partnerships—a crucial element of many of these practices—between financial institutions, businesses, and community-based organizations to build relationships with the immigrant community;
- Financial literacy, homeownership education, and counseling programs that contribute to sustainable homeownership for immigrants;
- Affordable loan programs;
- Training programs for loan officers and underwriters on how to measure immigrant creditworthiness in non-traditional ways; and
- Sweat equity programs that provide very-low-income immigrants with the opportunity to become homeowners through mutual self-help.

HOMEOWNERSHIP OPPORTUNITIES FOR HISPANIC IMMIGRANTS IN ROGERS, ARKANSAS

Rogers is a small town of 39,000, located in Northwest Arkansas. In 1990, very few Hispanics resided in Rogers, Arkansas. However, by 2000, Hispanics constituted almost 20 percent of the local population. Nearly all of these immigrants came to Rogers since 1993, attracted by the availability of work in the poultry processing industry as well as the quality of life in the community.

Not long after the arrival of significant numbers of Hispanic workers, Sam Walton, founder of the Wal-Mart Corporation and owner of the First National Bank in Rogers, inquired with the bank's President as to what the bank was doing for the newcomers. This catalyzed activity at the bank. Research conducted by the bank's community development officer revealed that the newcomers did not understand the U.S. credit system, basic banking, or how to get a traditional loan. This research also pointed to potential abuses of the immigrant population, due to a lack of a credit history, limited knowledge of the United States financial system, and limited proficiency in the English language. These factors often forced new immigrants to seek sources of high-cost financial services, such as nontraditional car loans.

FIRST NATIONAL BANK AND TRUST COMPANY

Founded in 1915, First National is the largest and oldest bank currently operating in Rogers. The bank was purchased by Sam Walton, founder of Wal-Mart Corporation, in 1975 and is now part of the Arvest Bank Group, of which the Walton family is primary shareholder. Other Arvest-owned sister banks are operated in adjacent communities; the holding company operates banks in northwest Arkansas, southwest Missouri, and central Oklahoma.

First National has a long history of providing support to the local school system, the chamber of commerce, and the local United Way chapter. Its senior management set an example by actively participating in charitable, service, and community organizations and encouraging similar involvement by all bank associates. The bank also established itself as an industry leader by offering new and innovative products. In 1976 First National was the first bank in Benton County to operate an automated teller machine and in 1998 it was among the first banks in the state to offer Internet banking. According to Federal Deposit Insurance Corporation (FDIC) call report data, First National's market share in Rogers ranged from 48.94 to 52.53 percent between 1994 and 1999. This market share has remained constant despite the appearance of several new financial institutions during the same period.

Member banks in the Arvest Bank Group subscribed to common principles of focusing on the customers' needs. Exploiting customers so that the banks can realize short-term returns was specifically addressed in associate orientation materials, and this practice was clearly and emphatically forbidden. As leaders in several communities, Arvest's banks strove more diligently than

(continues)

(*continued*)

many other financial institutions to offer services that appealed to all market segments. Because of this, First National was in a unique position; its product line contained services suited to and priced in a way to appeal to low- to moderate-income consumers, and the bank's associates underwent a minimum of 40 hours of training in recognizing customer needs and providing a high level of service to a diverse customer base. This combination made the bank appealing to consumers, especially those with limited language skills and financial resources.

In addition to finding the effects of predatory consumer lending in the immigrant community, the bank research uncovered a housing problem. When the first wave of immigrants arrived, Rogers lacked a supply of affordable rental property for these newcomers. The male population often lived in overcrowded conditions, particularly before family members arrived. Home ownership became a key opportunity to creating better housing conditions for both immigrants and their families.

FINANCIAL LITERACY SEMINARS

With this information, a bank task force decided to develop a financial seminar series titled "Creating Hope in the Work Place," to be taught in Spanish. Most of the newcomers had little formal education and no knowledge of the credit system in the United States. As more than one manager at First National pointed out, most bankers are too close to their profession and incorrectly assume that all consumers know how to do such basic transactions as writing a check, understand how bank accounts work, and have a basic trust in the banking system. Unfortunately, this is often not the case for newly arrived immigrants. Realizing that a lack of basic banking knowledge would frustrate both immigrant customers and bank associates, the bank developed a curriculum that provided a foundation of financial knowledge, including how to write a check, establish a credit history, buy a house, and plan for retirement.

First National purposely designed the seminars using simple concepts. The first seminar, covering basic banking services, introduced financial services and gave a brief overview of future seminars. Attendees were taught the very basics: the advantages of keeping money in the bank instead of at home, and the fact that no consumer has ever lost money on a U.S. government-insured deposit. The seminar on how to write a check included a pocket card, which translated the parts of the check ("Pay to the order of," "Memo," "Dollars") into Spanish, and gave examples of writing the date and the check amount in English. The size of this class was typically limited to no more than ten individuals, to ensure that the instructor was able to give adequate instruction to students as they learned to write out checks, fill out deposit slips, and use the automated teller machine (ATM).

Seminar instructors from the bank gradually introduced more complex financial topics as immigrants attended subsequent seminars. Topics such as buying a house offered the bank instructor an opportunity to extend an invitation to those interested in specific bank services to see him at the bank. While the seminars gradually covered more complex subject matter, the seminar materials still broke down the topics into basic, understandable terms. Probably the most effective example of this occurred in the retirement planning seminar, where the instructor illustrated how a worker can immediately realize a return of 50 cents for every dollar invested. How? The answer was not a highly speculative stock or mutual fund, but the employee's 401(k) plan, which offered a 50 percent employer match on contributions. The instructor knew that most of the immigrants were not participating in their plans because they did not understand them.

To gain the trust of the newly arrived immigrant audience, the bank determined that the seminar instructor needed to able to communicate in the workers' native language and be familiar with the audience's cultural and educational backgrounds. This measure helped the instructor to better explain the concepts included in the seminars, and enabled the audience to learn better. This strategy ultimately benefited the bank and the newcomers.

BANK-EMPLOYER PARTNERSHIP

Making this financial literacy information accessible to newcomers was not a small task. The greatest challenge was finding a time and place when the newcomers were most open to learning. The bank offered sessions in various locales, including churches, but ultimately put its most concentrated efforts in developing a partnership with a local employer of large numbers of immigrants.

The bank believed that the workplace provided the best time and place to ensure an attentive and interested audience. After a shift, workers were often too tired to learn, and on weekends they attended to family matters. Accordingly, the bank tried to convince employers why providing such seminars at the workplace would benefit them.

Aware of the high turnover costs for the poultry processing plants, the bank explained to employers that the workers would settle more permanently in Rogers if they understood and utilized the U.S. credit system, particularly to buy homes. That stable workforce would save the employer significant turnover costs, estimated at $3,000 to $4,000 per turnover. If the bank conducted the seminars at the workplace, employees would clearly see that the employer was trying to provide a direct form of help to them and their families.

The major employer that accepted the bank's offer to partner was North Arkansas Poultry. Starting in 1994, the employer provided classroom space for one-hour seminars scheduled during the workday. Management closed down the production line one section at a time to allow all workers to attend the seminars. To minimize effects of these shutdowns on monthly production, management tried to schedule seminars in production months containing five weeks (versus four weeks in most production months). To show their serious commitment to the value of the seminars and to encourage worker loyalty, the plant continued to pay the immigrant workers while they attended the seminars.

PREPARING THE BANK FOR THE IMMIGRANT MARKET

The bank recognized that educating the newcomers about the U.S. credit system was not the only obstacle that had to be overcome before the immigrants could start banking: the bank itself needed to be prepared to receive these new customers. First National prepared by training and hiring new staff as well as by developing new procedures to address the immigrants' financial experiences—or lack thereof:

Cultural training: Most bank employees had no previous experience with the Hispanic population. A community college professor was brought in to teach bank employees about the people they would be serving. His instruction addressed several fundamental questions about the newcomers: Where did the immigrants come from? What was rural Mexico like? Why were they in Rogers? How did they value family, church, and work? Why didn't they speak English?

Hiring bilingual staff: In addition to providing staff with training in survival Spanish, the bank hired bilingual tellers and loan officers. That was not an easy task in Northwest Arkansas, as the newcomers represented the first major group of Spanish speakers in the area. Initially, the bank hired the U.S.-born wife of a Mexican immigrant. Ultimately, the bank tapped various networks to find bilingual staff, including hiring bilingual high school students as interns; and tapping into the network of multicultural leadership throughout the region for recommendations about potential loan officers and tellers. One lesson the bank learned was that it is important to quickly and aggressively build a pool of potential bilingual candidates. This enabled the bank to select the very best from the beginning. By starting off with the very best, the non-Spanish speaking employees would hopefully understand that individuals were not hired for their language ability alone. In addition, any ethnic stereotypes would be quickly dispelled.

Essentially the bank found it more effective to train a bilingual person to be a banker than to teach a banker to speak Spanish. The majority of their bilingual staff began as tellers and learned the business from the ground up. Those that showed promise were then promoted to new accounts officers. Some later advanced to loan assistants, and three eventually became loan officers. Since the bank needed bilingual employees at a variety of levels somewhat quickly, promising staff was moved rapidly to higher levels of work.

As other banks in Rogers also developed an immigrant clientele, the demand for bilingual bank employees resulted in a very competitive market for such individuals. Tellers and loan officers trained by First National found a very good market for their skills at area banks. These banks clearly recognized their own need to prepare for providing services to the newcomers. To do so, they enticed away several officers trained by First National. The lesson the bank learned here was that good talent should never be neglected.

Developing alternative underwriting guidelines: The customary credit report did not fit the experience of many newcomers, who simply had no traditional credit history. To address this issue, the bank examined alternatives to traditional credit histories, which allowed loan officers to make loans decisions and anticipate what underwriters needed to know. For example, the payment histories for rent, utilities, water, and cable were used to supplement the traditional credit report. In addition, the bank used payment reports from used car agencies that typically accept installment payments only in cash, and do not report to the three major credit agencies in the United States.

Of the mortgage loans that First National made to recent immigrants, 90 percent were Federal Housing Administration (FHA) or similar types, such as U.S. Department of Agriculture Rural Development, Arkansas Development Finance Authority's Home Buyers Assistance Program, or Fannie Mae's Community Lending Program. Under FHA guidelines, a borrower cannot be turned down for having no credit history; instead, the guidelines emphasized employment stability and qualifying ratios (the ability to make payments based on income). In lieu of balances in bank accounts, cash on hand was also acceptable for payment of closing costs under FHA guidelines. In these instances, the bank asked the borrower to deposit the cash, and the borrower provided a letter explaining the cash and how it was saved.

While a credit history was not necessary, one full year of employment history was required to qualify for an FHA loan. This was easily achievable for many of the recent immigrants who applied for mortgage loans, since most were seminar participants with a stable work history in a local processing plant. However, the bank's underwriters noticed a number of circumstances where applicants were showing gaps in employment during the December holiday season. Lenders quickly realized the existence of a cultural practice where workers would quit jobs to go back to their native countries for the Christmas holidays, and then return to readily available jobs in the early part of the year. The bank's underwriters responded by annualizing income from the months in which the applicant worked. Employers also assisted with this dilemma by encouraging employees to take a leave of absence during the holidays instead of quitting. This emphasis on establishing a full year of employment history in the United States was of great importance, because in many instances, previous employment in other countries could not be verified.

Helping Immigrants Establish a Credit History: As mentioned earlier, one of the seminars taught consumers how to create a credit history. During the early stages of implementing this training, associates of First National quickly realized that many immigrants entering the local economy desired a way to establish credit. Naturally, First National hoped to attract new business from this hard-working population that generally had no previous credit experience. Among native-born citizens of the United States, young adults often establish credit by having a parent co-sign for a first loan, or by dealing with a banker with whom the family has established a relationship. However, in most cases neither of these options was available to the newly arrived immigrants served by First National.

Associates of the bank worked together to devise a creative, low-cost way for these consumers to develop a credit history, in a manner that carried almost no risk for the bank. At the end of the credit history seminar, the instructor explained that the bank offered a way to help consumers establish credit:

1. The borrower applies for a one-year, $1,000 term loan with monthly payments of approximately $85;
2. Funds from the loan ($1,000) are invested in a certificate of deposit (CD); and
3. The bank holds the funds in the certificate of deposit as collateral for the loan.

Note that this loan/CD arrangement did not require the bank to create a special product; rather, this arrangement was structured using existing, "off the shelf" banking services that First National already offered. Most bankers are averse to risk when dealing with unknown borrowers; however, the bank realized almost no credit risk on these loans since the CD was used as collateral. Because the CD earned interest, the net interest cost to the borrower was less than $15. By repeating this process twice, borrowers gained confidence in the lending process and in the banker, as well as met certain regulatory requirements for the FHA-type of home loans offered by the bank.

As it turned out, the major challenge in teaching the immigrants how to establish credit was correcting their desire to pay off the loan immediately. Unused to lending, many came to the bank in month two of the loan ready to pay off the entire loan. Bank officers ultimately convinced them of the value of the credit experience to their future financial activities.

LEADERSHIP AT THE BANK

Both the bank and the community faced several obstacles, including unfamiliarity with the conditions of an emerging immigrant community, a language barrier between immigrants and members of the larger community, and little understanding of the culture from which the immigrant populations came. All of these conditions created special circumstances that required the right persons to understand and overcome.

An important part of the success of First National's immigrant program was the commitment of "champions"—individuals with exceptional commitment. In this instance, both the bank's sales manager and the community development officer convinced bank management to support these activities and to commit other bank personnel to a range of tasks. This included:

- Bringing in experts to teach bank employees about Mexican culture;
- Designing the seminars;
- Convincing employers of the utility of the seminars;
- Teaching the seminars;
- Hiring and training bilingual staff to service immigrant customers; and
- Adjusting the bank's traditional ways of processing mortgage loans.

As these activities required considerable bank time and effort, these "champions" needed to initially convince management of the value of the seminars, and keep management behind this program at different points when the practice was being re-examined and refined. The commitment of bank management was essential. First, the program changed both key aspects of the bank's culture and its way of doing business. Second, significant resources were needed to carry out these services. Third, particularly in the context of a smaller community, long-held prejudices caused some valuable customers to resist the idea of the bank serving the financial needs of immigrants, particularly when the immigrants did not speak English or were minorities. This commitment was long term and required vision on the part of management.

Rob Brothers, president and CEO of First National Bank and Trust Company, Rogers, made it clear that while the bank saw an opportunity to benefit financially from the immigrant market, there was also a commitment to do the right thing. He gave several tests of what an institution must be willing to do to achieve the needed level of development:

1. A commitment of resources, particularly in terms of staff;
2. A willingness to reckon with cultural issues by sensitizing current staff to the customs and mores of the immigrant population;
3. The development of the staff's bilingual capacity as the market grows through the institution's push for expansion, developing staff with bilingual capacity; and
4. A long-term approach to profitability.

Early on, First National jumped enthusiastically into marketing to immigrants by conducting on-site survival Spanish lessons for bank employees (e.g., greetings, "deposit slip," "we need your signature on the back of the check"), and by launching an aggressive direct mail program. First National did some initial research and consultation with Hispanic market resources, and knew to avoid such common pitfalls as simply translating English-language advertisements into Spanish. However, the bank did indeed make mistakes, but quickly learned from them. For example, it was soon discovered that the key to communicating with Spanish-speaking customers was not to teach a new language to native speakers of English, as proficiency in a second language is difficult for many adults. Instead, the bank focused on hiring native speakers of Spanish with some knowledge of English as tellers and as loan staff. Attempts at identifying Spanish-speaking customers for direct mail lists proved to be mildly embarrassing to the bank's management, as some surnames assumed to be of Hispanic origin turned out to be Italian, while some Hispanic surnames belonged to families that had been in the United States for several generations. However, it is important to note that these setbacks did not cause bank management to abandon the effort; instead, they strengthened the resolve to refine the process into one that worked even better.

EMPLOYMENT AND HOUSING AVAILABILITY

While Rogers did not have an adequate supply of affordable rental housing for the newcomers, its homeownership costs were relatively low, particularly when measured against the annual income of immigrant workers. In the 1990s, most entry-level jobs in poultry plants earned between $8 and

$9 per hour, not including overtime, shift differential pay for night work, or other additional wages. Families followed the first wave of immigrant workers into the Rogers community, and in a good number of these families both adults worked in the same plant, taking different shifts to accommodate childcare needs. With dual incomes, these families often earned an annual income of $32,000.

Fortunately, the housing market in Rogers included an ample supply of small three bedroom houses, including new houses, with prices in the $70,000 to $85,000 price range. While still below the national average, real estate prices in Rogers have steadily crept upward as the area experienced tremendous population growth during the last 20 years. In some areas, land prices have doubled in the last decade. Most new houses built in the Rogers area were listed with real estate agents at prices well above $100,000, and it appeared that builders had little trouble finding buyers for these houses, given the average time that new houses stayed on the market. Builders might have ignored the needs of buyers wanting houses in a lower price range, given the healthy demand for more expensive houses.

But some builders in Rogers carved a niche in this lower end of the housing market, with excellent results. On the southern end of Rogers, for example, there was a small housing development containing perhaps 100 houses constructed in 1998 and 1999. Located along wide, winding streets and *cul-de-sacs* were quarter-acre lots with neat, well-maintained three bedroom homes covered in vinyl siding. The average house price in this neighborhood was approximately $75,000, which included land costs ranging between $8,000 and $10,000. Houses in this neighborhood proved popular with recent Hispanic immigrants not only due to their price, but also because the neighborhood's location was convenient to both schools and poultry processing plants. However, this neighborhood is far from being an ethnic enclave located "on the wrong side of the tracks." These houses also attracted a fair number of non-Hispanic buyers. Developers were quick to note the popularity of this area with recent Hispanic immigrants, and worked with real estate agents to modify their standard package to include features popular with this market segment:

1. Houses often had a master bedroom suite on a separate end of the living area from the other two bedrooms and bath, allowing more privacy for extended families;
2. Kitchens were equipped with gas ranges, which are more familiar to Hispanic buyers;
3. Paint and carpet colors were darker and brighter than in most homes of this price range, which usually feature "safe" neutrals;
4. Interior walls were finished in a stucco texture reminiscent of finishes often seen in Latin America; and

5. Houses were marketed by real estate agents who were culturally sensitive and familiar with loan programs tailored to low- to moderate-income buyers.

The experience of builders in Rogers proved that there was a viable, profitable market for houses tailored to newly arrived immigrant buyers, provided that builders were willing to adapt their product to the needs, desires, and price requirements of immigrant buyers. Again, the bank managed to offer financing without creating special loan programs or products, and instead used existing resources to serve low- to moderate-income buyers.

SUSTAINABLE HOMEOWNERSHIP

From 1994 to 2000, more than 700 immigrant families purchased houses for the first time through mortgages from the Arvest Bank Group (which includes First National). Many of these families bought their houses prior to 1997. In a pool of loans of this size, one expects a percentage of defaults approximating the community's average of around 4 percent; however, as of August 2004, none of these loans were in default.

Approximately half of the newly arrived immigrant buyers purchased newly constructed houses. As mentioned earlier, several new housing developments have been anchored and expanded by the infusion of investment from the immigrant community. In total, about 50 percent of the newcomers have become first-time homebuyers.

CAPTURING A NEW MARKET
AND INCREASED NEW BUSINESS

First National began its seminar series in September 1994. Based on information covering North Arkansas Poultry's 650-member workforce, only 8 percent of the poultry processor's employees were First National customers prior to the first seminar. Results were rapid and dramatic: after eight months and two seminars, 37 percent of the plant's employees were customers; and after two years, 60 percent were customers.

At the end of this two-year period, employees of North Arkansas Poultry had total deposits at First National in excess of $1 million, and it was not uncommon for immigrant workers to open accounts with initial cash deposits of $5,000 to $7,000. In addition, 7.4 percent of the employees had purchased houses with mortgage loans from First National with an average mortgage balance of $60,000, and 26.9 percent had consumer loans with the bank, with an average loan balance of $2,400. This growth and success is in spite of the fact that almost all of the immigrant customers of First National had not previously been customers of a bank.

While a certain percentage of any population either cannot or will not use banks, as of April 30, 1999, approximately 52 percent of the immigrants in Rogers were customers of First National, representing a total of $26.5 million in business:

- $5 million in deposit accounts;
- $1.2 million in consumer loans;
- $20 million in mortgage loans; and
- $341,000 in commercial loans.

Trends have indicated that the average deposit account balance has increased, and the immigrant customers have moved into new investment alternatives offered by the bank's investment and brokerage subsidiary, such as mutual funds, annuities and stocks.

First National's share of the immigrant homeownership business was directly related to the lender's seminars and preparation of the bank's associates to serve immigrant customers. Underlying the bank's success was the bridge of trust built between these new customers and the bank through the use of bank associates to both conduct seminars and assist immigrant customers with loan applications when they came into the bank.

During this period, First National's high satisfactory Community Reinvestment Act (CRA) rating for lending and service was due in part to the bank's work with the newcomer community. The regulators not only examined the bank's record at attracting low- and moderate-income business, but gave the bank additional credit for servicing the needs of underserved populations. In assigning the CRA rating, the regulators took into account the effort expended, the creativity required, and the results obtained from the effort. To ensure that the regulators understood the bank's efforts, First National took the examiner to the poultry plant in order to observe the seminar. The bank also took the examiner to visit the actual homes that newcomers purchased. The bank made sure that newspaper articles and other outside reports about the financial seminars and the bank's work with the new population came to the attention of the examiner.

While First National reaped considerable benefits from its approach to the new immigrant population of Rogers, the seven other banks in the city also benefited from the seminars. While these banks did not participate in the seminars, they gained a significant volume of new customers and issued hundreds of mortgages to the immigrants. The very fact that some hired bilingual staff away from First National (paying higher salaries to provide them with incentives to switch bank employers) demonstrates that other banks also saw a benefit to attracting immigrant customers.

SALT LAKE NEIGHBORHOOD HOUSING SERVICES

> Neighborhood revitalization is more than bricks and mortar. We can-
> not have strong and sustainable neighborhoods if we do not invest in
> stakeholders.

Established in 1977, Salt Lake Neighborhood Housing Services (NHS) is a private, non-profit corporation governed by residents, local businesses, and Salt Lake City officials. The organization unites resident adults, businesses and community leaders in an effort to provide affordable housing, build communities, and promote a positive image of target neighborhoods. NHS works with community partners to carry out its activities, and receives funding from many sources including banks, corporations, local businesses, private foundations, and individual donors.

The first-time homebuyer program at NHS assists low-income families, including immigrant families, who may not qualify for a home loan from a traditional lender. The program helps immigrants and other low-income individuals purchase a home in the NHS target neighborhoods; either an existing home or a brand new one built as part of the NHS construction program. A one-on-one counseling program guides customers through the home buying process. To ensure that families become successful homeowners, NHS requires potential homebuyers to participate in a minimum of eight hours of homebuyer education and learn the basics of purchasing and financing a home.

The training program begins with a one-hour *Homebuyer Orientation* meeting at the NHS office. At this meeting potential participants learn about available services and costs. They also complete a personal profile form to determine if they are eligible for the program. Qualified loan applicants must be U.S. citizens or permanent resident aliens with at least two-year employment history in the same line of work, and some ability to establish credit; for applicants with no established credit, NHS uses alternative sources of credit history, including rent and utilities payment history.

Participation in a *Home Buyer Education* course follows; participants learn about house hunting, credit, mortgages, and closing documents. The Home Buyer Education classes are free; however, a refundable deposit of $50 per person is required (the deposit is waived for NHS customers and participants in Salt Lake City's first-time homebuyer program). The deposit is refunded in full when NHS receives a copy of the HUD-1 Settlement Statement, which is one of the documents signed at closing.

To maximize the impact of its investments, NHS works with neighborhood residents to develop their leadership skills. Program participants learn how to get involved with city boards, advisory committees, and community councils, and participate in local events and activities that address neighborhood issues such as crime, gangs, street lighting, and traffic. Residents organize street festivals, town meetings, community surveys, cultural diversity workshops, and neighborhood revitalization activities. *Paint Your Heart Out* is NHS' most successful community revitalization activity. Once a year, volunteers paint the homes of senior citizens and/or disabled residents on fixed incomes. The exterior facelift helps preserve and beautify homes and contributes to community restoration and homeowner pride.

NEIGHBORHOOD DEVELOPMENT CENTER, TWIN CITIES, MINNESOTA

The already mentioned Neighborhood Development Center, Inc. (NDC), a community-based non-profit organization that works in the low-income communities of Twin Cities in Minnesota, currently partners with 18 neighborhood and ethnic-based organizations to provide, among other things, affordable housing to low-income African Americans, Hmong, and Latinos. Through the Real Estate Development Initiative (REDI) which commenced in 2002, NDC works with graduates of its entrepreneurship training program (see chapter 4) as well as neighborhood organizations to catalyze corridor revitalization in targeted neighborhoods, encourage property ownership and business growth among NDC's targeted entrepreneurs and enhance the capacity of neighborhood organizations to carry out real estate projects. NDC has capitalized a REDI Loan fund of $650,000 with loans from Wells Fargo Bank and Western Bank that it uses to provide a limited number of loans or equity investments to leverage projects in inner-city commercial corridors.

HOUSING SERVICES AT THE LATIN AMERICAN ASSOCIATION IN ATLANTA, GEORGIA

Based in Atlanta, Georgia, the Latin American Association is a non-profit organization that provides comprehensive transitional services for Latinos working toward self-sufficiency and an enhanced quality of life. Their mission is to respond to the Hispanic community's basic needs and help members gain the skills to fully participate in the larger community. Homeownership is a principal focus. The housing department assists families through seminars in Spanish on the home-buying process; an annual housing fair; landlord/tenant and rental counseling; credit, budget and banking counseling; and pre-purchase, post-purchase and default mortgage counseling. In 2005, the 9th Annual Housing Fair, presented by Washington Mutual, attracted over 850 people and representatives from 40 private and non-profit organizations in the areas of real estate, banking, insurance and housing law.

LAA is also working with Consumer Credit Counseling Service of Greater Atlanta and United Way of Metropolitan Atlanta to bring Atlanta's Latino community the opportunity to participate in the United Way's Individual Development Account (IDA) for Homeownership program. The aim is to offer this program in Spanish. The IDA program encourages low-income individuals to develop economic assets and matches their savings with community funds for a down payment on a home in a targeted neighborhood. IDA program families are provided the opportunity to address the major barriers to homeownership for low- and moderate-income families: a poor credit history, excessive debt, lack of savings for down payment, and lack of financial literacy and knowledge about homeownership.

NOTE

1. This section is based on two publications: Andrew I. Schoenholtz and Kristin Stanton, _Reaching the Immigrant Market: Creating Homeownership Opportunities for New Americans_ (Washington, DC: Georgetown University and Fannie Mae Foundation, 2001); Andrew I. Schoenholtz, "Newcomers in Rural America: Hispanic Immigrants in Rogers, Arkansas," in Elżvieta M. Goździak and Susan F. Martin, _Beyond the Gateway._

8

Community Development

Ethnic community development is a complicated measure of immigrant integration. Many researchers, policymakers, service providers, and community leaders focus on the importance of ethnic community development and community-based organizations (CBOs), which can be effective vehicles for serving immigrants. They are based within the newcomer communities and have the linguistic and cultural competency to reach many needy immigrants. Ethnic self-help groups and mutual assistance associations serve as intermediaries between newcomers and the host society, introducing immigrants to mainstream expectations and communicating ethnic interests to decision makers outside the immigrant community. Ethnic communities "cushion the impact of cultural change and protect immigrants against outside prejudice and initial economic difficulties."[1]

An overemphasis on ethnic community development, however, may be at odds with expectations and aspirations about social integration of immigrants into the broader U.S. society. Members of ethnic enclaves may integrate economically but not socially, supporting themselves without public assistance but remaining culturally isolated from mainstream society. The capacity and inclination to communicate with native-born U.S. residents and work alongside them to solve social issues are important marks of cultural and social integration. Reliance on ethnic communities, in other words, may not be conducive to social integration and civic engagement with the wider society.

Since the founding of the United States, ethnic communities have nevertheless played an important political and economic role in supporting the aspirations of their members. Confronted with the unknown, many newcomers seek out the familiar. They tend to live in close vicinity with other newcomers and shop at grocery stores that carry products from their home countries. Newcomer neighborhoods and businesses anchor a social support network that is vital to newcomers' well being and the achievement of early self-sufficiency. Most immigrants find employment, particularly the first job, through relatives and friends. Tightly knit ethnic enclaves are manifestations of immigrant entrepreneurship: employment within an ethnic enclave is often the best route for promotion into supervisory and managerial positions and for business ownership.

Indeed, behavioral science theory suggests that individuals who adapt bicultural modus operandi in the face of change—that is, retain their own cultural identity while incorporating elements of the new culture—are more likely to succeed than people who choose to assimilate completely, retreat to the familiar, or reject both the old and the new.[2] Our research indicates that integration involves a balancing of tendencies to retain the values, practices, and skills immigrants bring versus the pressure to adopt the norms and behaviors of the new society. Many successful integration initiatives identified by the research team blended the old and the new. Every locality visited in the course of this project displayed examples CBOs, mutual assistance associations (MAAs), or community development initiatives. The motifs for working together to facilitate integration of newcomers were quite diverse. So were the organizing principles. Most CBOs and MAAS were organized on the basis of common ethnic identity (e.g., the Khmer Aid Group of the Triad and the Montagnard Dega Association, both in North Carolina) or shared language (e.g., the Latin American Association in Atlanta). Most immigrants in the studied communities came from Mexico or Lain America and shared a common native language: Spanish. But the refugee communities, even those originating in the same continent or region, did not have the benefit of a lingua franca. Most refugee-led organizations were established instead on the basis of shared ethnic or tribal identity. In some instances, members of the same ethnic group with opposing political persuasions established competing organizations, which created further divisions within the community. The Somali Bantu in Atlanta, for example, appeared to have established at least two different community organizations.

CULTURAL COMPETENCY IN PRACTICE

Latinos make up the largest minority in Utah, over 224,000 strong. They represent 10 percent of the state's total population. Yet, few social service agencies, health care providers or government agencies have bilingual, biculturally competent staff to offer complete and effective service to Latino clients.

Centro de la Familia de Utah offers *Cultural Competency in Practice*, a program that provides training to service organizations to minimize language and cultural barriers and improve agencies' abilities to provide needed services for Utah Latinos. Thanks to a grant from the UPS Foundation, workshops are offered at no cost to participants, on a space-available basis. Culture-specific research, census data and other important practical information is provided to participants. This program strives to help clients identify and adapt to the unique demands of cross-cultural work. In 2003, the program provided training for 90 members representing 15 agencies in the Salt Lake City Metro area. Since then the program has grown; by 2005, over 2000 individuals participated in the training.

According to Community Affairs Manager Rebecca Chavez-Houck, the key to this program's success has been its cost-effectiveness in relation to local corporations' training budgets.

Umbrella Coalitions

Practices developed by umbrella groups or coalitions catering to diversified newcomer communities are promising engines of integration. Not only do they facilitate integration of newcomers into native U.S. society, they also foster linkages with other immigrant groups. In these instances, the linear integration process takes on new dimensions. Umbrella groups are organized on the basis of several different principles, including shared interest in a particular issue (e.g., domestic violence) or gender (e.g., refugee women). Two Atlanta-based examples are TAPESTRI, Inc., a coalition of community organizations serving domestic violence victims, and the Refugee Women's Network (RWN).

Immigrant and Refugee Coalition Challenging Gender-Based Oppression

The Immigrant and Refugee Coalition Challenging Gender-Based Oppression (or TAPESTRI, Inc.), a statewide coalition of ethnic—community-based organizations, aims to end violence against women, children, and the elderly in immigrant and refugee communities. The coalition was formed in 1994 by five agencies: the Center for Pan-Asian Community Services; Shalom Bayit/Jewish Family and Career Services; Raksha, Inc. for South Asians in Distress; the Refugee Family Violence Prevention Project; and Mercy Mobile's Latino Families at Risk. Three other agencies have since joined the coalition, whose name symbolizes the different threads of society coming together to cover and protect its many communities. Originally, TAPESTRI functioned as a project of the Refugee Women's Network, but in October 2002 it became an independent organization.

Currently, TAPESTRI is involved in many activities, including multicultural training, anti-trafficking, legal advocacy, domestic violence prevention, community education and political advocacy on behalf of women. Training in issues of domestic violence, sexual assault and human trafficking is provided for mainstream service providers, professionals and criminal justice system personnel. The organization also publishes The TAPESTRI Times, a bi-annual educational newsletter. TAPESTRI played a key role in establishing the International Women's House, a culturally and linguistically appropriate shelter for battered refugee and immigrant women. In 1997, the National Crime Prevention Council (NCPC) presented TAPESTRI with an award for a model project in crime prevention.

> A driver's license is a symbol of freedom. For a refugee woman, a driver's license allows her to become independent.
>
> —Arek Strzelecki

One of the leaders of TAPESTRI, Arek Strzelecki, has received a prestigious award from the Robert Wood Johnson Foundation's *Community Health Leadership*. The program supports community leaders tackling complex health problems by promoting healthy behaviors, violence prevention, mental health, community development and environmental health. Each award includes a grant of $120,000 to $150,000 for the leader's group and a $15,000 personal stipend. Arek chose to use these funds to establish yet another project for refugee women, *License to Freedom*, this time in San Diego, California. Arek stressed the importance of refugee and immigrant men getting involved in activities aimed at preventing and eradicating domestic violence in newcomer communities.

The Refugee Women's Network, Inc.

A national organization devoted to the needs of refugee women, the Atlanta-based Refugee Women's Network, Inc. (RWN) represents diverse ethnic communities. Two refugee women, Xuan Nguyen Sutter from Vietnam and Darija Pichanic from Bosnia, created the network in 1995 with a modest grant from the federal Office of Refugee Resettlement (ORR). Ten years later, the organization has an annual operating budget of $800,000, including funds from ORR, the Ford Foundation, the Annie E. Casey Foundation, the Community Foundation for Greater Atlanta, the Atlanta Women's Foundation, and many other private donors.

The network draws its strength, however, from the untapped human capital of refugee women resettled in the United States. Its programs include leadership training in community organizing, technical assistance to refugee women's groups, microenterprise, and health care education.

The *Refugee and Immigrant Women's Leadership Training Program* helps women become community advocates and problem-solvers. The training encourages refugee women to find strength in their united voices, participate at all levels of the society, and bring about changes that will benefit themselves and their communities. The program is based on "Training for Transformation," an approach to community development widely used in East and Southern Africa. It is adapted from Paulo Friere's teachings. Intensive and experiential, the approach emphasizes participant interaction, active listening, dialogue, action, and reflection with a minimum of lecture. The network has trained more than two thousand women residing in 35 states and representing 40 nationalities. Each year, several hundred refugee and immigrant women attend a national conference to share experiences and build alliances. More than 15 organizations nationwide have taken advantage of the network's technical assistance. In Dallas, an organization has raised funds to train refugee women in computer skills and childcare business. In San Diego and Sioux Falls, women have planned community centers, and in Arizona women started a family violence prevention program.

The *Micro-enterprise Project* was created in April 2001 at the request of participants in RWN's Leadership Training Program. In the first two years the program trained more than 160 refugee and immigrant women. The program's goal is to help women become economically self-sufficient through self-employment. Two types of business development training are provided, a six-week Business Plan Training and a six-session Family Child Care Business Training. Women are required to take part in the business plan training before enrolling n the childcare training.

The *Health Promoters Program* trains women in the Atlanta area to be health educators and liaisons between their communities and health care providers. This program is the result of a partnership between RWN, the Clarkston Community Center, and the DeKalb County Board of Health. The program aims to improve the health of refugee and immigrant families by educating participants about behaviors that promote health and improving access to community health care resources.

TOWARD A BROADER SENSE OF COMMUNITY

Despite the propensity to focus on one's ethnic community, newcomers interact with established residents in many different social arenas. Community boundaries are created through the exchanges between these groups in schools, workplaces, government offices, law enforcement, and health care facilities. It is this social space that fosters integration and change, on one hand, or isolation and conflict on the other. Successful integration often requires both newcomers and established residents to expand their notions of community.

Even among long-standing residents, establishing a sense of community is often a challenge. "Community" refers both to where people live and how they feel and act. In one sense, it evokes a feeling of collectivity that is linked to a specific geographic area or physical space such as a city, a town, a school, a place of worship, or a city block. In another sense, it transcends geographic limitations to unite a group of people sharing common behavioral patterns, values, and social ties related to traits such as ethnicity, religion, and nationality. It often takes time to feel comfortable when moving to a new city or town, entering a new school or changing jobs. This challenge is heightened for both newcomers and established community members when the newcomer's cultural and linguistic background is different from that of the majority.

Many localities create action plans to promote positive social interaction between newcomers and established residents and ensure that all residents receive quality service. These plans often emerge from the grassroots level as concerned residents, businesses, and public officials join forces to respond to rapid population change. In other instances, local governments take it upon themselves to create committees or task forces dedicated to incorporating all residents into community life. One approach is bottom up; the other is top down. The two often work in unison and can both be effective in solving challenges pose by rapid new settlement of foreign-born populations.

Winchester, Virginia: A Grassroots Approach

In Winchester, Virginia, a grassroots organization has effectively addressed the needs of the new Hispanic population vis-à-vis community institutions. The Latino Connection, founded in 1999 by a coalition of outreach workers, evolved into a networking and advocacy group that works on quality-of-life issues affecting the local Hispanic community. The group's mission is twofold:

- to coordinate efforts to provide culturally and linguistically appropriate services to Hispanic newcomers in Winchester and Frederick County; and
- to uphold the power of diversity in decision making by providing a forum to spread accurate, meaningful information among the newcomers, established residents, and community mediating institutions.

The Latino Connection is made up of thirty-five representatives from various community organizations, most of them involved in education and health care. These members, approximately half of them Hispanic, have permission from their employers to meet during regular working hours on a monthly basis for special initiatives targeting the Latino population. Valley Health System, a non-profit organization of health care providers, allows the group to use its facilities for meetings free of charge. That members of the Latino Connection are employed independently of the advocacy group allows it to remain informal—it has no paid staff and is not incorporated as a non-profit entity. This structure frees the group from worrying about its own economic preservation, allowing it to concentrate all its energy on issues related to the newcomer Hispanic population. By not seeking outside funds, the group also avoids stipulations that government regulations or private philanthropists might impose.

The Latino Connection's outreach and information initiatives focus on closing the gap between institutions unprepared for serving newcomers and immigrants unprepared for life in their new communities. In this sense their work is both "bottom up" and "top down" because it targets individual newcomers and the community institutions at their service. The group capitalizes on its members' standing employment with traditional mediating institutions such as schools, hospitals, and different sectors of local government. The arrangement allows members of the Latino Connection to provide information and resources directly to members of the newcomer community while simultaneously strengthening institutional capacity to meet newcomer needs through the education of colleagues.

Several of the founders of the Latino Connection are very well versed in the characteristics and needs of the agricultural migrant community through their involvement in the pre-existing Migrant Services Council as well as other citizen groups.

> An enemy is one whose story we have not heard.
>
> —Gene Knudsen Hoffman
>
> The justice is the harvest reaped by peacemakers from seeds sown in the spirit of peace.
>
> —James 3:18

The modus operandi for the Latino Connection has been to coalesce around a particular task or issue and follow through until a satisfactory solution is reached. The first task undertaken by the group was a community needs assessment based on the Quaker (Religious Society of Friends) Model of Compassionate Listening developed by Gene Knudsen Hoffman, a Quaker Peace Activist.

Compassionate Listening is a unique tool for reconciliation. Gene Knudsen Hoffman, a Quaker (Religious Society of Friends) peace activists writer, and therapist developed this tool after realizing that all parties in a conflict were wounded and needed to be heard. Her overarching principle is that hearing each other's story reveals unhealed wounds and allows for mutual compassion and understanding. Compassionate Listening is based on Quaker Universalistic spirituality. It helps to build bridges between individuals and communities in conflict and can ultimately lead to reconciliation.

The Latino Connection in Winchester, VA, used Compassionate Listening to design and conduct a community needs assessment. Faced with an influx of Latino immigrants who settled in the late 1990s in Winchester, a small city of approximately 25,000 primarily Caucasian and African American residents, Latino Connection understood the need to bring about appreciation and acceptance of the emerging population diversity to avert potential conflicts between Latino newcomers and established residents.

Indeed, Winchester was not a stranger to strained relations between immigrants and established residents. In 1999, an undocumented Jamaican migrant shot at point-blank a Caucasian police officer. And although the widow arranged for food baskets to be delivered to several immigrant families in Winchester in a show of solidarity with the newcomers that were blamed for the crime, the community remained divided over the issue of increased crime rates in the city attributed to newcomers.

The needs assessment identified access to and quality of Adult ESL classes as an area in need of improvement, including permanent, central location of the ESL classes; competency-based curriculum with pre- and post-assessment that allowed students with different language skills to progress accordingly; and availability of childcare services during class time. The coalition spent several months revamping the Adult ESL program before moving on to the next issue, namely perinatal care for immigrant expecting mothers.

Chamblee, Georgia: A Community Consensus Approach

The experience of Chamblee, Georgia, a small Atlanta suburb in DeKalb County, exemplifies the benefits and hardships that rapid population growth can bring. A widely publicized case in 1992 illustrated the challenges that can emerge as a result of newcomer settlement. Residents complained about Hispanic men who gathered on a street corner to be picked up for day labor, accusing them of stirring trouble and using private property as a dump. At a city council meeting, officials suggested using bear traps in residents' yards to discourage the men from trespassing. These comments came in the wake of the remarks by Chamblee's police chief that the "problem will continue until these [foreigners] go back where they came from."

The council meeting sparked a tense community-wide debate that was eventually settled by a conflict resolution team from the U.S. Department of Justice. Chamblee changed course and began to actively seek newcomer settlement and investment, attracting immigrant businesses that have revitalized the economy. In 1999, Chamblee's community development director put it clearly: "If the immigrants hadn't come, Chamblee would look like a bombed-out, 1950s American dream, complete with empty strip malls and abandoned buildings." Today Chamblee has higher tax revenues and a vibrant economy that capitalizes on its international flavor.

The engine for Chamblee's growth has been the city's International Village District. Home to more than five thousand immigrants representing at least twenty-five different ethnic groups, the International Village is one of the most diverse areas in the country. A partnership among the city of Chamblee, DeKalb County and the DeKalb Chamber of Commerce, the Village is an ongoing redevelopment of four hundred acres immediately north of the DeKalb Peachtree Airport. The commerce chamber formalized the concept in 1992, calling for a "village" that would become a nucleus for a growing international community within the greater metropolitan area. The village was to be a home, workplace, learning center, tourist center, retail center, and recreation area for individuals and businesses with a variety of cultures. Chamblee developed a long-range master plan in 1994, formalizing plans for a pedestrian-friendly area with mixed-used opportunities, retail, and related developments. At a three-day public workshop, city residents stressed a desire to maintain the residential land use component within the village, the importance of public open spaces, and the appeal of a self-sustaining community that, on its own, would attract businesses, residents and tourists.

Over the next five years, the city witnessed significant redevelopment of properties, including preparations for the International Village Cultural and Community Center (IVCCC). The plan for the IVCCC consisted of development of a community daycare center in a first phase and a cultural center in a second phase. The city renovated a condemned apartment complex with funds from a federal block grant and essentially donated it to the nonprofit group in charge of developing the community center, leasing it for $10 a year.

In early 1999, ground was broken for a $3 million, seventeen thousand-square-foot childcare center in the International Village area. The facility, which was constructed in less than a year, is a testament to the prioritization of the needs of the area's diverse population. Affordable childcare had long been a major need in Chamblee. The new facility, known as the Sheltering Arms Center, offers childcare for low- to moderate-income families

who pay based on their earnings. Anonymous donations paid for $2 mil-
lion of the construction costs. The completion of the first phase of the project has permitted the facility to serve 140 children from approximately
thirty-six countries, speaking more than thirteen languages.

The plans for a recreation and cultural center call for office space for non-
profit social service agencies and a performing arts center. This second
phase of the project was still being designed, but Chamblee officials passed
special zoning rules to control development and drive the International Village Project forward. Officials razed several rundown apartment complexes
and renovated others, and they were trying to persuade entrepreneurs to set
up shop in the district. Plans for the district include shops, restaurants and
a cultural and community center. While the primary goal remains assisting
the local multicultural population, village boosters hope their development
will draw tourists and locals who aren't aware of the diversity in the international corridor. They estimate it could draw more than three hundred
thousand tourists a year, with annual retail sales of $160 million.

Greensboro, North Carolina: "Community Learning" Model at Guilford College

In another example of community development, Guilford College, founded
by Quakers, is one of five colleges in Greensboro, North Carolina, that provide opportunities for students to work with immigrants and refugees. The
college describes the emphasis on hands-on work as "community learning,"
the accomplishment of tasks that meet human needs while fostering educational growth. Students involve themselves through courses with service
components, service-oriented internships, and alternative projects during
school vacations.

Guilford students have worked directly with the immigrant population
through placements with community-based organizations such as the Montagnard Dega Association, the Center for New North Carolinians at the University of North Carolina Greensboro, the Buddhist Center, and the Glenwood Library. The Montagnard Dega Association is a non-profit organization
established not only to help resettle the Montagnards of Greensboro, but also
to advocate for the freedom the Montagnard population that remains in Vietnam. Students help with after school programs, tutoring programs, grant writing, elderly outreach, and youth programs. Other organizations enlist students for similar service projects that engage the immigrant population.

NOTES

1. Alejandro Portes and Rubén Rumbaut, *Immigrant America: A Portrait* (Berkeley:
University of California Press, 1990), 88.

2. John W. Berry, "Cultural Relations in Plural Societies: Alternatives to Segregation and Their Socio-psychological Implications," in *Groups in Contact*, ed. N. Miller and M. Brewer (New York: Academic Press, 1984). See also Dan A. Chekki, "Beyond Assimilation: The Immigrant Family and Community in a Canadian Metropolis" (paper presented at the Congress of the Humanities and Social Sciences, Canadian Sociology and Anthropology Meetings, Halifax, Canada, June 1–4, 2003).

9

Cultural and Religious Heritage Preservation

Cultural traditions and histories provide an important touchstone for immigrant communities to preserve their sense of self for the next generation. For some communities, sharing their reach histories and celebrating native heroes have also represented key strategies for teaching mainstream society about their backgrounds. One way of accomplishing this goal is the promotion of cultural heritage preservation activities. Almost every locality we visited during the course of this research organized public festivals and celebrated ethnic holidays: Chinese New Year, *Cinco de Mayo*, and others. Many also established "weekend schools" to teach immigrant children their native languages or folk dancing. The Buddhist Temple in Greensboro, for example, has a very vibrant dance group performing traditional Khmer dances. Every April, the Cambodian New Year celebration draws hundreds of people to the temple. Together they share their prayers, honor their elders, and take pride in their Cambodian heritage. They invite American friends to join the celebration and to learn about Khmer traditions.

"WE REMEMBER, WE CELEBRATE, WE BELIEVE": A PHOTO HISTORY OF LATINOS IN UTAH

In 2000, Armando Solórzano, an ethnic studies professor in Utah, started gathering oral histories among Latinos from different socioeconomic, religious, occupational and national backgrounds. He gathered more than two hundred interviews, which touch on family structure, social attitudes, work history, cultural practices and gender roles. In a companion photo exhibit, Solórzano chronicled Latinos' past and current involvement in the state.

The exhibit, titled "We Remember, We Celebrate, We Believe: A Photo History of Latinos in Utah," comprised fifty-two large photographs organized around themes with commentary in Spanish and English. It opened with a ceremony at the Utah State Capitol Rotunda in 2002 and has traveled to other Utah universities, to California and abroad.

Solórzano hopes the exhibit will promote diversity, increase Latinos' visibility and humanize their experiences. "Latinos are an integral part of Utah," Solórzano says. "We were here even before the pioneers. We need to be seen. We just want to be treated as equals and as humans." The photographic images, collected from individuals, organizations, families, friends, archives and the Utah State Historical Society, each depict a story about Latinos' contributions to Utah. The frames capture Latinos' contributions to the surging sheep industry in Monticello, their influence in the establishment and growth of the Catholic Church and The Church of Jesus Christ of Latter-Day Saints, and their work in Utah mines and railroads. The final frames depict more recent activities, including Utah Latinos' successful campaign to name a Salt Lake City street after César Chávez, leader of the first successful U.S. farm workers' union.

When asked to discuss her history, one elderly Latina told Solórzano, "I have none—only photographs." So precious were these pictures, many of their owners, rather than loaning them to Solórzano, insisted on accompanying him to the copy store to reproduce the images. "For some Latinos, the photos were the only remaining memories they have of their family and of their people. When I touched these photos I felt like I was touching something sacred," he said.

TOU GER XIONG:
MULTICULTURAL, MULTILINGUAL, MULTICOOL

> As much as we are different, we are alike in many ways. We have no other choice but to get along.
>
> —Tou Ger Xiong

Tou Ger Xiong bills himself as the world's first Hmong storyteller and rap artist. He was born in Laos in 1973, but his family left after the communist takeover in 1975, seeking refuge in a Thai refugee camp. His family immigrated to the United States as refugees of war four years later, and Xiong began his childhood in America in the public housing projects of St. Paul. The valedictorian of his high school, he enrolled at Carleton College in Northfield, Minnesota where he developed a passion for the performance arts. He created *Project Respectism*, an educational service project that uses comedy, storytelling, and rap music to bridge cultures, which he presented to schools, churches, colleges and community groups throughout the Midwest while writing his thesis.

Since Xiong graduated from college with a degree in political science, *Project Respectism* has evolved into a program that provides cultural entertainment, or "preservation education," for people of all professions and backgrounds. Xiong has taken his message of respect to thirty-five states in the past six years. He has given over eight hundred presentations nationwide to audiences of all ages and ethnic backgrounds, sometimes reaching as many as eight thousand people in a week.

GREENSBORO BUDDHIST CENTER

In North Carolina, the Greensboro Buddhist Center, mentioned several times in this handbook, has become an invaluable resource for the local Lao and Khmer communities. Organized in 1985 by the Khmer Aid Group of the Triad with help from Lutheran Family Services and a grant from the Z. Smith Reynolds Foundation, the center is located on ten acres that includes two houses. The rural setting enhances its serene atmosphere and provides ample space for religious, cultural, and educational activities for over 500 families from North Carolina, South Carolina and Virginia. The congregation is made up primarily of Lao and Cambodian refugees and their families. The temple, which provides culturally appropriate mental health services for traumatized refugees, helped forge a viable ethnic and religious enclave that attracted other Buddhists. The Triad area is now home to about fifteen hundred Cambodian refugees and more than one thousand Laotians with multiple small businesses and communities of faith.

A range of Buddhist ceremonies are held annually at the Greensboro Center, including celebrations of Buddha's Birthday, Southeast Asian New Years, and Kathin, when the monks are offered new robes. Each week the Greensboro Buddhist Center holds a service beginning at nine o'clock. Up to two hundred regular members attend and stay for lunch, dharma lessons, and recreation. The temple holds larger monthly services in Thai, Lao, or Cambodian traditions that attract four or five hundred devotees. Led by the three resident monks, the services include chanting of the sutras and offerings of food to the monks. Although the monks speak English, the services are held in Lao or Khmer. Translators are available for these languages and the center also offers language classes.

During the week, the monks offer classes in Buddhism and lecture at local schools. The temple also sponsors two dance groups as well as a summer camp for children. Members of all ages enjoy the lake, volleyball court, and gardens located behind the worship site. One key to the success of this ethnic spiritual center was a gifted community organizer. A Thai Buddhist monk who spoke Khmer, Lao, Thai, and English came to serve at the Greensboro Buddhist Center in 1989. The monk served as a well-spoken representative of the refugees for the general population and was well-liked within the community.

ST. MARY OF THE ASSUMPTION CHURCH IN PARK CITY, UTAH

While many refugee and immigrant communities establish their own places of worship to preserve their culture and religious traditions, mainstream religious organizations have taken an integrated approach to worship. Beyond merely sharing worship space, as religious institutions have done across the country, these efforts have incorporated newcomers into standing practices. Some 2,500 Latino immigrants, mostly from Mexico, attend St. Mary of the Assumption Church in Park City, Utah. A turning point in the history of the parish came with the arrival of the icon of Our Lady of Guadalupe, commissioned by a local Mexican couple for the new parish church. Fr. Robert Bussen, pastor of St. Mary's, remembers showing the gift to congregants who attended the English Mass. They nodded and pronounced it "beautiful." However, when he unveiled the large, gilded icon to his Latino congregation, they fell to their knees and started praying. The Latino dedication ceremony of the new church included a four-mile procession with community members carrying the icon down Park City's Main Street. To this day, the icon draws a steady flow of worshipers. A multitude of flowers and candles attests to its importance for the local Latino Catholics. The icon is both a religious as well as a national symbol; it is a sacred image that unites Mexicans and offers comfort and a sense of belonging.

"FROM CAMBODIA TO GREENSBORO: TRACING THE JOURNEYS OF NEW NORTH CAROLINIANS"

This exhibition, created by the Greensboro Historical Museum, Inc., the City of Greensboro, and the Center for Documentary Studies at Duke University in collaboration with the Greensboro Buddhist Center, attempts to provide the host community a better understanding of the experiences of one significant group of immigrants in the Greensboro area—the Khmer of Cambodia. Through photos, artifacts and personal and historical narratives, the exhibition educates visitors about the history, culture and traditions of Cambodia, and Khmer approaches to spirituality and community. The exhibit is also available online.[1]

NOTE

1. http://www.greensborohistory.org/cambodia/index.html.

10

Legal Assistance and Community Security

Early on, newcomers need help learning their new rights and a new set of laws. Understanding and obeying laws and mores of the new homeland is critical to successful integration. Without this knowledge, immigrants are vulnerable and have no sense of security and belonging. Several projects set out to provide newcomers with the necessary assistance.

THE BRIDGING THE GAP PROJECT, INC., ATLANTA

Bridging the Gap's (BTG) mission is to "improve the quality of life in Georgia's ethnically diverse communities by forming partnerships that overcome cultural barriers and promote understanding between residents, law enforcement, educators, and other service providers." Toward this end BTG coordinates translation and interpretation services including interpretation for courts, law enforcement, attorneys and social service providers. Through its New American Services program, BTG provides immigration-related services including immigration photos, fax and copy services, notaries, and financial services such as ATM and money order sales. This "one-stop shop" model simplifies the immigration process by pulling together tools for all the small tasks that might otherwise seem overwhelming to immigrants with limited knowledge of English or of required legal procedures.

MINNESOTA ADVOCATES FOR HUMAN RIGHTS'
REFUGEE AND IMMIGRANT PROGRAM, MINNEAPOLIS

Minnesota Advocates for Human Rights is a volunteer-based, non-governmental, non-profit, 501(c)3 organization dedicated to the promotion and protection of human rights. Founded in 1983, the organization has more than 4,000 members, including more than 600 active volunteers.

The Refugee and Immigrant Program seeks to promote and protect the human rights of refugees, asylum-seekers, and immigrants. Projects of the Refugee and Immigrant Program include the Refugee and Asylum Project, the Legal Advice Clinic Project, the Minnesota Detention Project and the Minnesota Asylum Project.

Program activities include documenting human rights abuses, advocating on behalf of individual victims, educating on human rights issues, and providing training and technical assistance to address and prevent human rights violations. Minnesota Advocates has produced more than 50 reports documenting human rights practices in more than 20 countries; educated over 10,000 students and community members on human rights issues; and provided legal representation and assistance to over 3,000 disadvantaged individuals and families.

The Refugee and Asylum Project provides free legal representation to indigent asylum seekers who have fled or are in danger of persecution, torture or execution if forced to return to their home countries. The project recruits and trains volunteer attorneys, paralegals, and law students to represent individuals who have fled religious, ethnic, political, or gender-based persecution in their countries of origin. Using a large pool of volunteers, the Project provides *pro bono* representation to hundreds of individuals each year.

Through the Legal Advice Clinic Project Minnesota Advocates co-sponsors four local walk-in legal clinics that provide immigration legal advice and referrals to residents of Hennepin County, MN. The Park Avenue Foundation/Volunteers Lawyers Network Walk-in Legal Clinic assists low-income residents of Hennepin County who do not have legal counsel, and serves more than 300 low-income residents of Hennepin County every year. The Center for Families North Minneapolis Walk-In Legal Advice Clinic provides one-time consultations for advice and referrals. Since 2002 Minnesota Advocates staff has also been providing legal advice in immigration matters to persons referred by the Minnesota AIDS Project through the Minnesota AIDS Project Legal Advice Clinic. Finally, another partnership with the Center for Victims of Torture has provided torture victims with legal advice about asylum and related matters at the Center for Victims of Torture Legal Advice Clinic.

The Minnesota Detention Project provides brief consultation and representation to immigration detainees in Minnesota. Through the efforts of volunteers from the legal community, Minnesota Advocates provides consultations and representation to all immigration detainees at their initial appearances in Immigration Court. This is the only opportunity for the vast majority of the hundreds of non-citizens detained by immigration authorities in Minnesota to meet with an attorney prior to their removal hearings. The Minnesota Detention Project is supported in part through funding by the Department of Health & Human Services, Administration for Children & Families, Office of Refugee Resettlement and by Lutheran Immigrant & Refugee Services/Presbyterian Disaster Assistance.

Minnesota Advocates also supports asylum-seekers by providing free expert medical and psychological evaluations and testimony in support of asylum claims through the Minnesota Asylum Network. This program provides training to volunteer medical and mental health professionals who then provide expert assessments and testimony in support of asylum seekers. Minnesota Advocates partners with the Center for Victims of Torture and Physicians for Human Rights in providing this program.

CASA GUADALUPE, GREENSBORO

Casa Guadalupe was created in 1990 as an outreach program of Catholic Social Services to serve the Hispanic population of the Piedmont Triad area. In 1990, a United Way of Greater Greensboro grant supported the establishment of satellite office in Greensboro, NC offering general and immigration services. The program aims to meet basic human needs and support civil rights through its immigration work and advocacy on behalf of the Hispanic community in the Piedmont Triad area. To accomplish this, *Casa Guadalupe* provides direct general and immigration services and acts as a referral engine to other service agencies in the area.

Casa Guadalupe operates out of two locations, in Winston-Salem and Greensboro. The Greensboro office offers general services Monday–Friday 9am–3pm and Immigration Services on Monday 10am–2pm. Immigration services include access to two Board of Immigration-accredited representatives that handle client cases, including representation at the local Board of Immigration office and Immigration Court. *Casa Guadalupe* also maintains a network of immigration attorneys for referral and can help clients interact with the Mexican Consulate in Raleigh, NC, and BCIS in Charlotte, NC. Interpretation is available at doctor's offices, nearby state or federal agencies, court or anywhere the need arises. Other services include document translation; help with basic tax forms and referrals for services that are not provided directly.

PREVENTING CRIME AND
PROMOTING COMMUNITY SECURITY

As newcomer populations grow, challenges arise from diverging expectations about appropriate social behavior. Lack of familiarity with local laws and cultural barriers can generate misunderstandings between established residents and newcomers that lead to the involvement of law enforcement. For example, in some countries large groups of people commonly gather on weekends to drink beer, socialize, and play soccer. However, established residents in some communities find these gatherings inappropriate or threatening, even if no laws are being broken. In a society with diverse behavioral norms, newcomers find themselves treading unfamiliar waters. Language barriers only aggravate the frustration of both newcomers and law enforcement.

Crime and victimization concern everyone, but they have an especially devastating impact on newcomers. Many immigrants fear and mistrust the police because of traumatic experiences with uniformed officials in their native countries. Newcomers and police departments alike must work together to overcome mutual feelings of mistrust. Two programs, one in Atlanta, and the other in Park City, Utah, have significantly improved relations between newcomers and the law enforcement community. The newly appointed Chief of Police in Winchester, Virginia, has created a new immigrant community liaison position and is initiating a series of new efforts to work with the local Latino community.

The Bridging the Gap Project, Inc., Atlanta

The Atlanta-based Bridging the Gap (BTG) Project is based on the idea that the biggest integration challenge for immigrants stems not from racial barriers, but from misunderstandings related to cultural diversity. At the time of our research, the project used three primary strategies to reduce those misunderstandings: a crisis intervention program; an education initiative for immigrants, landlords, and law enforcement officials; and a youth program. It began in 1994 with the sponsorship of institutions including the U.S. Department of Health and Human Services' Office of Refugee Resettlement, the U.S. Department of Justice's Community Oriented Policing Services and the Governor of Georgia's Children and Youth Coordinating Council.

New American Services Program

Under the New American Services Program (NASP), BTG was working to facilitate some of the technical stages of integration. A one-stop center developed by the program would distribute immigration forms, take immigration photographs, issue money orders, register newly naturalized Americans to vote, provide passport applications, and refer customers to legal counsel for assistance. The NASP operates in conjunction with offices of the U.S. Immigration and Naturalization Service (INS) in Atlanta and Charlotte, North Carolina.

Crisis Intervention and Police Program

The crisis intervention and police program was initiated to respond to 911 calls from non-English speaking callers. BTG employed more than twenty staff members, speaking fifteen different languages, to take calls on a special hotline and notify emergency responders. The program aimed in part to reduce a perception among immigrants that police were hesitant to enter their communities. As part of the project, BTG works with law enforcement agencies to recruit personnel from diverse cultural populations.[1]

Community Oriented Policing and Education Program[2]

> COPE has been and will continue to be a great help to our officers simply because the communities began talking to us and began to trust us as police officers more than they did in the past.
>
> —A. Smyrna, Georgia, police officer

Atlanta law enforcement agencies believed that many service providers did not fully understand the difficult tasks faced by peace officers. Service providers and law enforcement felt also that each could be more sensitive to the challenges of the other. To solve this problem, law enforcement requested that BTG form the Community Oriented Policing and Education Program (COPE).

With COPE, law enforcement served as the primary partner in a collaborative effort to provide crime prevention information to refugee and immigrant communities. The program provided a range of education and outreach services to ethnic communities, local law enforcement agencies, social service providers, corporations, and schools.

The COPE program was divided into three central initiatives:

- Recruitment of bilingual and bicultural interpreters and translators, volunteers, and bilingual and bicultural applicants for careers in law enforcement.
- Outreach activities for Haitian, Korean, Laotian, Latino, Somali, Chinese, and Vietnamese communities, which consisted of

  1. convening Community Enrichment Training (meetings for immigrants and law enforcement to share information and solve problems together);

2. monitoring five language-specific telephone hotlines for reporting criminal activity;
3. creating and distributing community orientation materials in six languages;
4. participating in ESL courses to assist in opening lines of communication with law enforcement; and
5. furnishing employment and service referrals, as needed.

- Services for law enforcement agencies

1. Provide law enforcement agencies with access to COPE-operated Community Outreach Centers. At these centers law officers were able to meet with refugees and immigrants and discuss crime prevention issues and operate programs such as gang intervention and violence education.
2. Provide interpretation and translation services, particularly during follow up on crime incidents.
3. Develop community oriented policing strategies.
4. Provide Peace Officer Standards and Trainig POST certified training for law enforcement on diversity, use of interpreters, and race relations.
5. Assisted Atlanta area Asian police officers in establishing the Asian police Officers' Association.

COPE resulted in an enhanced communication between law enforcement and immigrants. Refugees and immigrants began to trust law enforcement. For instance, in one gang-ridden neighborhood that previously lacked a law enforcement presence and where COPE specialist was threatened on a daily basis, residents started to participate regularly in community meetings with law enforcement. In addition, the outreach worked began getting requests for information and assistance instead of threats. Three neighborhoods developed neighborhood watches and tenant associations. COPE recruited 94 bilingual and bicultural citizens for positions in law enforcement agencies.

There were also many challenges. Refugees' lack of trust in uniformed authorities was an obstacle in many communities. Since COPE served five county metropolitan area where many different languages are spoken it required a substantial investment in staff. COPE had 15 full-time staff members fluent in 12 languages and more than 180 volunteers providing interpretation and translation in 78 languages. However, for smaller communities or those where fewer languages are spoken, the program is easily separated into components so it can be implemented according financial resources of a given agency.

Mediation Project

Mediation between landlords and immigrants has been another focus of the project. The community outreach division convened meetings to educate

ethnic communities about life in the United States and help them build relationships with mainstream social service providers. The project also provided employment referrals for immigrants and implemented translation
services so that immigrants can better interact with government institutions.

THE YOUTH PROGRAM

Finally, BTG developed a program to target immigrant youth because they
are involved in many of the crimes reported to the hotline. The youth program featured support groups, a newsletter and a truancy prevention program. An annual "Youth Challenge Day" brought ethnic youth together
with law enforcement officers to participate in sports activities and educational workshops. Another initiative provided conflict resolution and diversity training to young leaders at a high school plagued by hate crimes.

Funding Challenges

Unfortunately, non-profit funding dried up in 2003 as the economy
struggled; by 2004, BTG had lost most of its grants and it verged on closing
its doors. The crisis intervention, landlord liaison and youth programs were
victims of the shortfall. To cope with the changes, BTG reduced the number
of paid staff from 28 to five, and changed their business model from grant-
funded non-profit to fee-for-service.[3] The organization contracted with the
federal immigration service to provide travel and visa forms to the public
and began providing basic services such as copying and photography and
form translation. A contract was also established with the Georgia Department of Human Resources to provide translation services to refugees. This
adaptive strategy has allowed BTG to survive and continue providing essential services to Atlanta's immigrant population.

The Community Outreach Program of the Park City Police Department, Park City, Utah

In Park City, Utah, an upscale resort community an hour from Salt Lake
City, the demand for low-wage service workers skyrocketed in the late 1990s
amid a booming economy and preparations for the 2002 Winter Olympics.
An influx of Latinos, mostly Mexicans, met the demand, but posed new
challenges for the police department. An inability to engage the newcomers
because of language and cultural barriers strained officer morale. Some local business and residents began to express fears about the new population.
Confusion over their relationship with INS (now Immigration and Customs Enforcement) also complicated matters.

Realizing that the newcomers were there to stay, police Chief Lloyd Evans
concentrated on proper service provision instead of fruitless deportation
efforts. Considering they could be victims, complainants, or witnesses, he

wanted newcomers to have access to basic services. Frustration over an inability to communicate pervaded the police ranks and required immediate attention. A series of public forums helped Evans identify key problems confronting local law enforcement and the needs of newcomers. Recognizing a need for a liaison between the newcomers and the police, the department created a community advocate position. The idea was for a figure to encourage newcomer trust and use of police department resources, teach newcomers how law enforcement operates in Park City, implement a newcomer community crime prevention program and act as a point person for the community at large.

With the community outreach program, the Park City police stressed that immigration status was not their main concern. Racial profiling was denounced and a police accountability program was set into motion. The community liaison has access to the police chief and all police reports dealing with the newcomer population. Another series of public forums on concerns regarding the police ensured the participation of the wider community.

The Diversity Outreach Program has now been in operation for seven years and provides liaison services, advocate services and basic information/language assistance services to non-English speaking members of the community. The Outreach Program has received national recognition for its methods in developing and maintaining working partnerships with the police and the immigrant community.[4]

While language barriers and funding still pose a challenge, the program has successfully addressed community needs. Newcomer communities now have the strongest neighborhood watch programs in Park City. The program enjoys the support of local elected officials, has assuaged concerns from the established community vis-à-vis newcomers, and has added its voice to those advocating state and federal legislation to improve relations between newcomers and law enforcement.

In 2003, Shelly Weiss, the Hispanic Community Liaison for the Park City Chief department traveled to the Shenandoah Valley to conducting a training for local law enforcement on working with new immigrants. Chief Evans followed up her visit in 2004 to share his experiences with representatives of Latino Connection and the Winchester Police. The message brought to Winchester regarding the need for community outreach and liaison with the new immigrant community did not go unheeded. The following section highlights the creation of Winchester's Community Outreach Coordinator position, a representative of the local government who works with the new immigrant community.

Community Outreach Coordinator, Winchester, Virginia

In 2006, the City of Winchester in Virginia created a community outreach coordinator position within its government structure to work with local government and the new immigrant community on issues related to language access, trainings, and community outreach. The most pressing issue is language access and the current outreach coordinator has made substantial progress in developing an on-call schedule for trained interpreters to aid with government-immigrant interactions. The Winchester Police are involved in and support this initiative.

In the area of community outreach and education, the coordinator has worked with the Hispanic Outpost of the Salvation Army to establish a monthly networking meeting of local Latino pastors. The outreach coordinator has taken advantage of this forum by bringing in speakers each month from community services agencies to provide information to these community leaders for them to share with their respective congregations. Representatives from the local police and the department of motor vehicles have presented at the meetings. The overall goal is to build confidence within the Latino population as it relates to the local government and the police department, so that we could successfully and effectively provide further outreach efforts such as a bilingual citizens academy or neighborhood watch program.

In an attempt to improve the way information is being shared with the community, the outreach coordinator work closely with ESL department in the public schools to share information on city issues and provide public transit advice to parents. They have developed a bilingual community newsletter that is created with content from the police and the City government.

NOTES

1. See the manual "Safety and Crime Prevention Manual for Immigrants" at http://www.btgonline.org for more information on educating newcomers about public safety.

2. Discussion of COPE is based in part on the description of the program found in *Powerful Partnerships. Twenty Crime Prevention Strategies That Work for Refugees, Law Enforcement and Communities,* developed by the National Crime Prevention Council.

3. Craig Schneider, "Agency Finds a Way to Survive," *Atlanta Journal-Constitution,* April 8, 2004.

4. http://www.parkcity.org/citydepartments/police/community/index.html.

Conclusion

Now the hard work begins. If this handbook is successful, it will save communities and institutions from "reinventing the wheel." However, as community leaders and service providers affirm, these ideas require dedicated staff and serious effort to become successful programs. The results—economic, social, and cultural integration—make this hard work well worth the effort.

It is up to all the actors—newcomers, established residents, policy makers, community leaders, service providers, educators, law enforcement, and a multitude of other community members—to erase the divided social worlds that mask relations of domination and inequality between newcomers and established residents. Programs and policies must focus on participation and membership within programs and institutions aimed at facilitating immigrant integration and opportunities to pursue shared, concrete tasks. Local initiatives must seek to transform neighborhood activities and organizations to mobilize both newcomers and established residents. National strategies need to support these building blocks.

Appendix: Contacting the Promising Practices

ARKANSAS

Arvest Bank Group
Arvest Bank—Rogers, AR
P.O. Box 809
Rogers, AR 72757
(479) 621-1775
http://www.arvest.com/banking/

GEORGIA

The Bridging the Gap Project, Inc.
77 Forsyth Street, Suite 100
Atlanta, GA 30303
(404) 581-0044
http://www.btgonline.org

International Village District
(770) 458-6660
http://www.internationalvillage.com

Latin American Association
2750 Buford Highway
Atlanta, GA 30324
(404) 638-1800
http://www.latinamericanassoc.org/
index.asp

Plaza del Sol
5522 New Peachtree Rd.
Chamblee, GA 30341

Refugee Healthcare and Medical
    Mentorship Project
Lutheran Services of Georgia
1330 West Peachtree St.
Suite 300
Atlanta, GA 30309
(404) 875-0201
(800) 875-5645
http://www.lsga.org

Refugee Women's Network
    (RWN), Inc.
4151 Memorial Drive
Suite 103 F.
Decatur, GA 30033
(404) 299-0180
http://www.riwn.org

TAPESTRI, Inc.
PMB 362
3939 Lavista Road, Suite E,
Tucker, GA 30084
(404) 299-2185
www.tapestri.org

MINNESOTA

Building Immigrant Awareness and
Support (The B.I.A.S. Project)
Minnesota Advocates
for Human Rights
650 3rd Ave. S, #550
Minneapolis, MN 55402
(612) 341-3302
http://www.mnadvocates.org

Center for International Health
640 Jackson St.
Saint Paul, MN 55101
(651) 254-1900

Centro Legal, Inc.
2610 University Ave. W, Suite 450
St. Paul, MN 55114
(651) 642-1890
http://www.centro-legal.org

International Institute
of Minnesota
1694 Como Ave.
St. Paul, MN 55108
(651) 647-0191
http://www.iimn.org

Lincoln International High School
730 Hennepin Ave.
Minneapolis, MN 55403
(612) 872-8690
http://www.lincolnihs.org

Mercado Central
(612) 728-5485
http://www.mercadocentral.net/
pages/1/index.htm

Minnesota Advocates
for Human Rights
650 3rd Ave. S, #550
Minneapolis, MN 55402
(612) 341-3302
http://www.mnadvocates.org

Neighborhood Development
Center
63 University Avenue, Suite 200
St. Paul, MN 55104
(651) 291-2480
http://www.ndc-mn.org

Tou Ger Xiong
8455 Ashford Road
Woodbury, MN 55125
(651) 738-0141
tougerxiong@comcast.net
http://www.gohmongboy
.com/hp.asp

University of Minnesota
Extension Research/Outreach
Center
1605 160th St. W
Rosemount, MN 55068
(651) 423-2413

NORTH CAROLINA

Casa Guadeloupe
2201 West Market Street
Greensboro, NC 27420
(336) 574-2837
http://www.cssnc.org/casaguadalupe

Center for New North Carolinians
413 S Edgeworth St.
Greensboro, NC 27401
(336) 334-5411
http://cnnc.uncg.edu

"From Cambodia to Greensboro:
Tracing the Journeys of New
North Carolinians"
Greensboro Historical Museum
130 Summit Avenue
Greensboro, NC 27401
(336) 373-2043
http://www.greensborohistory.org

The Greensboro Buddhist Center
2715 Liberty Rd.
Greensboro, NC 27406
(336) 272-1607

Guilford College
5800 West Friendly Ave.
Greensboro, NC 27410
(336) 316-2301
http://www.guilford.edu

Immigrant Health ACCESS
  Project (IHAP)
Center for New North Carolinians
413 S Edgeworth St.
Greensboro, NC 27401
(336) 334-5411
http://cnnc.uncg.edu

Glenwood Library
1901 West Florida Street
Greensboro, NC 27403
(336) 297-5000
http://www.greensboro-nc.gov/
Departments/Library/default.htm

St. Mary's Catholic Church
1414 Gorrell St.
Greensboro, NC 27401
(336) 272-8650

Our Lady of Grace Catholic Church
2205 West Market St.
Greensboro, NC 27403
(336) 274-6520
http://www.olgchurch.org

UTAH

Centro de la Familia de Utah
3780 South West Temple
South Salt Lake, UT 84115
(801) 521-4473

Even Start Family Literacy Program
5190 Heath Avenue (5030 West)
Salt Lake City, UT 84118
(801) 646-5095

Horizonte Instruction
  and Training Center
1234 South Main Street
Salt Lake City, UT 84101
(801) 578-8574
http://www.slc.k12.ut.us/sites/
horizonte/

Park City Municipal Corporation
P.O. Box 1480
Park City, UT 84060
(435) 615-5000
information@parkcity.org
http://www.parkcity.org/
citydepartments/police/
index.html

People's Health Clinic
P.O. Box 982342
Park City, UT 84098
(435) 615-7822
www.peopleshealthclinic.org

Salt Lake Neighborhood
  Housing Services
622 West 500 North
Salt Lake City, UT 84116
(801) 539-1590
http://www.slnhs.org/pindex.html

"We Remember, We Celebrate, We
  Believe: A Photo History of
  Latinos in Utah"
Armando Solorzano
University of Utah
Dept. of Family and Consumer
  Studies and Ethnic Studies
  Program
(801) 581-5168
armando.solorzano@fcs.utah.edu

VIRGINIA

Healthy Families of Northern
   Shenandoah Valley
301 North Cameron Street
Winchester, VA 22601
(540) 536-4113

Latino Connection
333 West Cork Street
Winchester, VA 22601
(540) 536-5435
http://latinoconnection.us

Northern Shenandoah Valley
   Adult Education
156 Dowell J. Circle
Winchester, VA 22602
(540) 667-9744

Partners in Perinatal Care
333 West Cork Street
Winchester, VA 22601
(540) 536-5435

Promotoras de Salud
Blue Ridge Area Health
   Education Center (AHEC)
MSC 9009

James Madison University
Harrisonburg, VA 22807
(540) 568-3383
http://www.brahec.jmu.edu/
promotoras.html

Winchester Public Schools ESL
(540) 667-4253
http://www.wps.k12.va.us/
specprogs/esl/eslhome.htm

CONTACTING
THE GEORGETOWN
UNIVERSITY TEAM

Elżbieta M. Goździak
(202) 687-2193
Emg27@georgetown.edu

Micah N. Bump
(202) 687-2401
bumpm@georgetown.edu

Institute for the Study of
   International Migration
Georgetown University
3300 Whitehaven St. NW
Suite 3100
Washington, DC 20007

About the Author

Elżbieta M. Goździak is director of research at the Institute for the Study of International Migration (ISIM) at Georgetown University and editor of a peer-reviewed journal International Migration.

Micah Bump is a research associate at the Institute for the Study of International Migration. He is also the associate editor of the journal, *International Migration*. He holds an M.A. in Latin American Studies with a certificate in refugee and humanitarian emergencies from the Graduate School of Foreign Service at Georgetown University.